REAL FAST
INDIAN
FOOD

REAL FAST
INDIAN
FOOD

MRIDULA BALJEKAR

metro

This edition published in 2002 by Metro Publishing Ltd,
3 Bramber Court, 2 Bramber Road London W14 9PB

All rights reserved: no part of this publication may be reproduced, stored
in a retrieval system, or transmitted in any form or by any means,
electronic, mechanical, photocopying or otherwise, without the prior
written consent of the publisher.

© 2002 Mridula Baljekar

Mridula Baljekar is hereby identified as the author of this work in
accordance with Section 77 of the Copyright, Designs and Patents Act
1988.

Illustrations by John Mansbridge

British Library Cataloguing in Publication Data. A CIP record of this
book is available on request from the British Library.

ISBN 1 84358 020 9

10 9 8 7 6 5 4 3 2

Typeset by Wakewing, High Wycombe, Buckinghamshire
Printed in Britain by CPD Group, Wales

CONTENTS

INTRODUCTION 7

THE BASICS 11

A GUIDE TO INGREDIENTS 20

SOUPS, STARTERS & SNACKS 27

FISH & SHELLFISH 47

CHICKEN & TURKEY 63

LAMB & PORK 95

VEGETARIAN DISHES 115

SALADS & VEGETABLES 135

BREADS, CHUTNEYS & RAITAS 159

MICROWAVE RECIPES 181

SWEET TREATS 195

MENU PLANNER 207

SUPPLIERS OF INDIAN INGREDIENTS 217

INDEX 219

A Note to Cooks

Preparation times are a guide to making and cooking the recipes, but do not include freezing, standing or chilling, where necessary.

Where a guide to microwave cooking is given, times are based on using a microwave with an 850-watt output.

Introduction

'Indian food, authentic and fast? Impossible – it's a joke!'

I would not blame you for questioning the concept of speeding up proper Indian cooking, because you would be right to be sceptical before looking at this book!

With the demands of today's busy lifestyles, spending time cooking and preparing meals for the family, or when entertaining, is becoming more and more difficult. Sometimes it is also easy to forget about the nutritional value of everyday meals. Never before have we had such a wide variety of ingredients from which to select and this ever-increasing choice of foods can make shopping bewildering. However, many foods are intended to make life that little bit more convenient – ingredients from around the world not only are available but are often sold prepared and ready to cook. Meat and poultry can be bought trimmed and diced; vegetables washed, chopped and ready to serve in salads; there is also a terrific array of spices and spice pastes for adding instant flavour when cooking. Although I prefer to prepare ingredients myself, these convenience products can be very useful when, in addition to doing a day's work outside the home, we play the roles of family chauffeur, housekeeper, cook and cleaner.

Creating attractive and delicious Indian dishes is not as time-consuming as is generally believed. It is possible to cook a nutritious and visually appealing Indian meal without spending hours in the kitchen. In fact, you can present a wonderful feast within an hour or less! The trick is to combine a little organization with a few simple, but vital, steps to success. Once you have mastered this, you will be amazed how quickly you can invalidate the idea that Indian cooking is complicated and lengthy.

A Little Organization

By this, I do not mean an entire change of lifestyle. All it involves are four simple principles.

1 Always keep the storecupboard well stocked.

2 Have the ingredients accessible, next to the hob or oven, before starting to cook.

3 Have the cooking utensils and all other equipment within easy reach.

4 Read the entire recipe and make sure that you understand it fully before you start preparing the food or cooking. Not only will this save time, but it also helps to prevent mishaps.

Key Steps to Success

The following will help you to succeed with speed.

1 Use pre-blended spices (see page 14) whenever possible. Spending a few minutes blending and storing spices appropriately cuts down preparation and cooking time when you are making a meal. This is particularly useful when you are preparing a meal for friends, as they would like to spend time with you, not just catch the occasional glimpse of your apron!

2 Either buy or make your own ginger and garlic purées (see page 16). Preparing small amounts of ginger and garlic can be comparatively time-consuming, so spending a little time to prepare a large batch of these frequently used basic ingredients will cut down the effort involved in making individual meals. Both purées can be kept in the refrigerator for up to 15 days or they can be frozen for up to 6 months.

3 Use one of the three cook-ahead sauces (see page 16) to create a delicious curry in a hurry. If you want to buy prepared curry sauces and pastes, then add a few spices of your own to enhance their flavours. Generally, a few whole spices, such as cinnamon, cardamom, cloves and bay leaves, will transform a bought product. These should be added to the oil first and cooked

briefly. Then add fresh herbs, such as coriander and mint, and use fresh chillies and tomatoes as appropriate.

4 Have hot water ready to add to a dish. This is important in Indian cooking not only to retain the flavours of the carefully blended spices, but also to enhance them, making all the difference to the flavour of the finished dish. Remember to put the kettle on to boil while you prepare the ingredients. It is also quicker to add hot water when cooking rice, rather than waiting for the water to boil in the pan.

5 Take advantage of all the time gaps between the different stages of a recipe. For instance, while lentils or meat are simmering, start preparing the ingredients for the next dish. Frying onions is probably the most time-consuming step in an Indian recipe as it can take up to 15 minutes to cook them properly. Remember, you do not have to attend to them constantly, but can get on with another part of the recipe or another dish in the meantime.

6 When you are cooking dry dishes, such as kababs (kebabs), make double the quantity and chill or freeze half for future use. Kabab mixes can be prepared in seconds in a food processor and you can create an entirely new dish by cooking the second half of the batch with one of the sauces you will already have in the refrigerator or freezer.

7 Leftover meat and poultry dishes can be transformed into a new meal by turning them into instant pilaus. Simply mix them with boiled basmati rice and garnish with fried onions or toasted nuts. All you need is a raita and some pappadums to complete the meal.

8 For side dishes, as far as possible make raitas as they do not need cooking and take only a few minutes to prepare. With the right combination of ingredients they are tasty as well as nutritious.

9 If you have a microwave, make use of it for the many Indian dishes that can be cooked very successfully by this method. For example, the microwave is great for cooking rice – simply start it off, then forget about it. This is also a practical method for par-cooking potatoes and other vegetables before spicing them up in a jiffy on the hob.

10 A pressure cooker is another useful piece of equipment. Lentils and beans can be pressure cooked in less than half the time taken for boiling. Add the *tadka* (the seasoning mix) to transform plain cooked pulses it into a delicious dish. Lentils cook in 7–8 minutes in a pressure cooker and potatoes can be cooked in a separate dish (with a little water added) at the same time. Cut the cooked potatoes into bite-sized pieces and toss them in hot oil with a few spices.

11 Use canned beans and peas to save time. They work very well if they are drained and rinsed thoroughly first.

12 Peeling vegetables can take time. Since most of the nutrients are found immediately under the peel, I often choose young vegetables and new potatoes which do not need peeling. Carrots are the exception as they are best peeled (even the baby ones) to remove traces of chemicals. To ensure that the flavours of the spices penetrate unpeeled vegetables, make small incisions through the peel or prick them with a fork before cooking. Making small incisions also cuts the cooking time slightly.

13 Lastly, choose cuts of meat that cook quickly and buy them ready diced or cut them into small bite-sized pieces to reduce the cooking time. Similarly, cut vegetables into small bite-sized pieces which cook more quickly than large chunks.

Now you are fully prepared to challenge the taste buds with exotic, highly nutritious and superbly flavoured food which does not demand hours of preparation and cooking.

This is my way of taking Indian cooking into the new millennium – I hope you will find it useful and that it will be a source of pleasure for years to come.

Bon appétit.

The Basics

Putting my idea of organization into action is not difficult. Identifying the useful basic ingredients and making sure you keep them in stock, in their most useful form, will help to speed up shopping, food preparation and cooking. From ensuring the storecupboard is full of useful ingredients to having a stock of prepared spices and sauces, setting aside time occasionally to top up the supply of essentials is not as time-consuming as starting from scratch every time you cook an Indian meal.

Stocking the Storecupboard

When you live a busy life, a well-planned storecupboard is an absolute necessity – and remember that the freezer is also the modern extension of the traditional storecupboard.

Pappadums and Pickles

Have at least two varieties of pappadums. It is more economical to buy the uncooked pappadums and they will keep for 3–4 months in an airtight container (I use a biscuit tin). They can be cooked under a hot grill or in the microwave in a few seconds. I include plenty of recipes for raitas, pickles and chutneys, but a few jars of bought pickles and chutneys will save time and add instant interest to your meals. They are usually good quality, so you can buy them with confidence.

Breads

Although making bread takes time, chapatis are relatively easy to make and the prepared dough can be stored in the refrigerator for 2–3 days. If you keep it any longer, it will darken on the surface owing to oxidation, but this is not harmful. Cooked chapatis can be frozen and reheated on a hot griddle with a little oil or butter.

I find that bought puff pastry makes excellent parathas, and because of the large amount of fat in the dough I do not use fat when cooking them. Roll out the pastry and cut it to size, then roast the breads on a hot griddle – the result is delicious.

Keep bought naan, chapatis, pitta and other breads in the freezer. I have included hints and tips on how to jazz these up as well as on reheating them successfully to achieve a soft, fluffy texture. Soft wheat-flour tortillas are very much like chapatis; the only difference is that they are made with plain flour instead of the wholewheat flour (*atta*) used for chapatis. Tortillas are excellent for wrapping kababs, adding relish, to make a quick meal. The tortillas can be frozen and used as required.

Rice
Basmati rice is easy to cook if you follow the recipes precisely; however, it does need soaking, even if only for 15–20 minutes. Easy-cook basmati rice does not need soaking, but it takes slightly longer to cook and does not have the unique aroma of traditional basmati.

Spices
It is a good idea to visit an Indian store at least once every 3–4 months to stock up on spices; then you will never have to worry about finding the right ingredient in your local shop. Resist the temptation to buy extra-large packs – although whole spices will retain their flavour for at least 12 months, ground spices quickly diminish in flavour. Many Indian shops provide a mail order service and I include a few useful names and addresses on page 217.

Canned Foods
Every storecupboard should include a range of canned foods, including tomatoes and pulses, such as chick peas, kidney beans and black-eyed beans. These are quick and easy alternatives to dried pulses. Canned fruit in natural juice is an excellent base for quick desserts to round off mid-week meals.

Prepared Spices
For fast and efficient cooking, set aside a little time (perhaps over a weekend) to prepare some basic ground spices and spice mixtures. Roasting and grinding the spices brings out the volatile oils they each contain, which give them their flavours. When preparing spice mixtures, roasting the seeds together mixes the volatile oils to give the ground-spice mixture the best flavour.

Ground Roasted Cumin

Cumin seeds have a warm, assertive pungency without being harsh and roasting them gently enhances these characteristics. Once roasted and ground, cumin will keep far longer in an airtight container than the fresh seeds and the spice is ready for use in many different ways. For instance, it will enliven plain roasted or grilled meat and poultry, fried or roasted potatoes and salads.

Preparing, grinding and storing cumin correctly will give you perfect results every time. Preheat a heavy-based pan (preferably cast iron) over gentle heat and roast the seeds until they release their aroma. This usually takes 40–60 seconds. Take care not to overheat the seeds as this will dry out the volatile oil and, in turn, impair the flavour. Cool the seeds slightly before grinding them in a coffee grinder. Then cool the ground spice completely before storing it in an airtight container, away from direct light.

The amount to make depends on how often you use the spice. Generally, I do not prepare more than 225g (8oz). I suggest you make about 125g (4½oz) at first and from the time it takes you to use this amount, judge your requirements in future.

Ground Roasted Coriander

Follow the same method as for Ground Roasted Cumin. This sweet and mellow spice is particularly good with chicken, fish and vegetables. Besides using it where suggested in the recipes, you can sprinkle ground roasted coriander on grilled fish and poultry with confidence as it contributes an excellent flavour.

Five-Spice Mix

This is a combination of five aromatic seeds that together create a unique flavour. A light seasoning of this mix will add loads of flavour to vegetables, pickles and lentil dishes. Even if you do not use any other spices you will achieve a wonderfully aromatic dish simply by frying a teaspoon of this mixture in hot oil and adding it to the food once it is cooked. You can buy five-spice mix from Indian stores, where it is known as *panch phoron*, but, if you already have all the individual spices, you can easily mix it yourself.

Mix 1 teaspoon each of black mustard seeds and onion seeds with 2 teaspoons each of cumin seeds and fennel seeds. Add ½ teaspoon fenugreek seeds and mix well. Store in an airtight jar away from direct light.

Three Useful Spice Blends

This method of preparing spices results in a superior, unbeatable flavour and it also prolongs the shelf life of the spices. These blends will delight you with spectacular results for 3–4 months, depending on how frequently you use them. They will remain fresh for 6 months when stored in an airtight jar, away from direct light.

If you are preparing food for young children, omit chilli powder from the spice blends. Chilli powder or fresh chillies can be added to a dish once you have removed the children's portions. The chilli should be cooked into the dish before it is served, so cook the dish briefly for 2–3 minutes after the chilli has been added.

Follow this simple method to prepare all three spice blends. Use a cast-iron or other heavy-based pan to roast the spices briefly before grinding them in a coffee grinder. Preheat the pan over a medium heat for about 1 minute. Add the spices and reduce the heat to low. Roast the spices gently for the suggested time (this depends on the particular spice mix). Immediately they are roasted, transfer the spices to a plate or bowl to prevent them from over-roasting on the heat of the pan. Allow to cool before grinding and storing.

VEGETABLE AND POULTRY SPICE BLEND

This is suitable for all vegetable and lentil dishes, and some poultry and game recipes.

MAKES 75G (2½ OZ)

30g (1oz) coriander seeds
15g (½oz) cumin seeds
7g (¼oz) fennel seeds
2 tablespoons ground turmeric
½–1 tablespoon chilli powder (optional)
1½ tablespoons garam masala

- Following the instructions on page 13, roast the coriander, cumin and fennel seeds for 2 minutes, stirring continuously, then allow to cool.

- Grind the cold spices, then stir in the turmeric, chilli powder (if using) and garam masala until thoroughly mixed.

MEAT AND PULSES SPICE BLEND

Use this blend for delicious results with lamb, pork and dried pea or lentil dishes.

MAKES 75G (2½ OZ)

30g (1oz) coriander seeds
15g (½oz) cumin seeds
1½ teaspoons black peppercorns
5 bay leaves, cut into small pieces
12 cloves
seeds from 8 brown cardamom pods
2 x 5cm (2in) pieces cinnamon stick, broken
1 tablespoon ground turmeric
½–1 tablespoon chilli powder (optional)
2 teaspoons dried mint

- Roast the coriander and cumin seeds with the peppercorns, bay leaves, cloves, cardamom seeds and cinnamon for 2 minutes, stirring continuously, then allow to cool.

- Grind the spices finely, then add the turmeric, chilli powder (if using) and mint, and mix thoroughly before storing.

FISH AND SEAFOOD SPICE BLEND

As its title indicates, this spice mixture is ideal for fish and seafood dishes.

MAKES 75G (2½ OZ)

30g (1oz) coriander seeds
15g (½oz) cumin seeds
7g (¼oz) fennel seeds
1 tablespoon aniseeds
1 tablespoon ground turmeric
½–1 tablespoon chilli powder (optional)

- Roast the coriander, cumin and fennel seeds with the aniseeds for 2 minutes, stirring continuously, then allow to cool.

- Grind the roasted spices and mix thoroughly with the turmeric and chilli powder (if using).

Two Essential Purées

Garlic and ginger are frequently used in Indian cooking; they are also so delicious in all sorts of other dishes that it makes sense to save time by preparing them in large batches.

Garlic Purée

Peeling and crushing fresh garlic hardly takes any time, but for convenience, purée a large batch of peeled garlic cloves in a blender or processor and store the purée in a suitable airtight container in the refrigerator or freezer. You can, of course, buy ready-made garlic purée, but the home-made version always has a superior flavour.

Ginger Purée

Use a potato peeler to peel fresh root ginger or, if the ginger is very young and covered by fairly thin, fine peel, scrape off the peel with a small, sharp knife. A grater is the easiest piece of equipment for preparing the ginger. Do not use the finest blade as the ginger simply sticks to it; instead try the blade with medium or large serrations. Store the grated ginger in an airtight container in the refrigerator or freezer. You may even prefer to buy the ready-made version.

Cook-Ahead Sauces

Ready-to-use sauces are real time-savers. Although there are all sorts of different sauces on the supermarket shelves, there are only three types of basic sauce in Indian cooking, and ingredients are added to these three basic sauces to create a variety of dishes. In strict culinary terms, sauces are often identified incorrectly. For example, 'korma sauce' and 'tikka sauce' are named according to the style or technique of cooking the food with which they can be served rather than the method by which these sauces have been prepared or the ingredients they contain.

Here you will find three basic sauces to use as the base for a host of different dishes. These sauces can be stored in airtight containers in the refrigerator for 10–12 days or they can be frozen for up to 8 months. When freezing, divide the sauces into 300ml (½ pint) quantities.

If you are cooking for young children, omit the chillies from the sauces. When reheated, once you have removed the portions required for children, add chilli powder to taste to the remaining sauce and be sure to simmer the sauce for a further 3–4 minutes.

A word of warning! Do not taste the sauces on their own and base your opinion on that flavour – they are designed to have a good flavour when combined with other ingredients.

MADRAS CURRY SAUCE

This makes a wonderful base for many well-known and popular Indian dishes. Curry leaves are not generally sold in the supermarkets, so look out for them in specialist shops. They lend such a distinctive flavour to this sauce that it is worth making a trip to an Indian store to buy them. The fresh leaves can be frozen, or bought dried leaves will keep well for at least 6 months in an airtight jar away from direct light.

MAKES 1.2 LITRES (2 PINTS)

---

5 tablespoons sunflower oil or vegetable oil
55g (2oz) fresh root ginger, peeled and roughly chopped
16 large garlic cloves, roughly chopped
8–10 shallots, roughly chopped
2 tablespoons fresh curry leaves or 3 tablespoons dried curry leaves
1½ tablespoons ground cumin
2–3 teaspoons chilli powder
2 teaspoons ground turmeric
85g (3oz) tomato purée
1.2 litres (2 pints) lukewarm water
2½ teaspoons salt or to taste
1½ teaspoons sugar
15g (½oz) fresh coriander leaves and stalks, chopped
3 tablespoons lemon juice

- Heat the oil over medium heat and fry the ginger, garlic and shallots for 3–4 minutes, stirring continuously. Add the curry leaves, cumin, chilli powder and turmeric. Fry gently for 2–3 minutes, then stir in the tomato purée. Cook for 1 minute before pouring in the water. Stir in the salt and sugar. Bring to the boil, reduce the heat to low and cover the pan. Simmer for 20 minutes.

- Add the coriander leaves and lemon juice. Simmer for 1 minute and remove from the heat, then leave to cool. Process the sauce until smooth in a blender. Store in an airtight container in the refrigerator or freezer.

BUTTER SAUCE

This sauce is ideal for a whole range of dishes, including korma, pasanda, and chicken tikka masala. Dried fenugreek leaves add the unmistakable flavour and aroma that are typical of this sauce. (The dried leaves keep well for 8–10 months when stored in an airtight jar away from direct light.) If you have a spice infuser, use it to hold the whole spices, saving the time and effort involved in removing them individually from the cooked sauce; alternatively, tie the spices in a piece of muslin.

MAKES 1.75 LITRES (3 PINTS)

---

3 x 5cm (2 in) pieces cinnamon stick, broken up
6 brown cardamom pods, bruised
10 cloves
4–5 green chillies, seeded if liked
2 x 400g (14oz) cans chopped tomatoes
140g (5oz) tomato purée
1 tablespoon Ginger Purée (see page 16)
1 tablespoon Garlic Purée (see page 16)
2 teaspoons sugar
2 teaspoons salt or to taste
1–2 teaspoons chilli powder
600ml (1 pint) warm water
2 teaspoons dried fenugreek leaves (*kasoori methi*)
225g (8oz) butter, cut into lumps
240ml (8fl oz) double cream

- Put the cinnamon, cardamoms and cloves in a spice infuser or tie them in a piece of muslin and place in a saucepan. Add the chillies; tomatoes with their juice; tomato, ginger and garlic purées; sugar; salt and chilli powder. Stir in the water and bring to the boil, then reduce the heat to low and simmer, uncovered, for 30 minutes.

- Remove the whole spices and purée the sauce in a blender. Return the sauce to the pan and stir in the fenugreek leaves, butter and cream. Simmer for 10 minutes, then leave until cold. Store in airtight containers in the refrigerator or freezer.

NORTHERN CURRY SAUCE OR KADHAI SAUCE

Ideally, this sauce is meant for bhuna *dishes, which are stir-fries, usually cooked in a* kadhai, *the Indian equivalent of a wok. It can be added to dishes cooked in a sauté pan or frying pan.*

MAKES 1.4 LITRES (2½ PINTS)

4 tablespoons sunflower oil or vegetable oil
675g (1½lb) onions, roughly chopped
55g (2oz) fresh root ginger, roughly chopped
13–14 garlic cloves, roughly chopped
2 teaspoons salt
2 teaspoons sugar
1½ tablespoons coriander seeds
4–5 dried red chillies (long slim variety), chopped
400g (14oz) can chopped tomatoes
1 tablespoon paprika
1 teaspoon ground turmeric
900ml (1½ pints) warm water
2 teaspoons dried fenugreek leaves

- Heat the oil in a saucepan over medium heat. Fry the onions, ginger and garlic for 5–6 minutes and then add the salt and sugar. Cook for a further 4–5 minutes, stirring regularly.

- Meanwhile, coarsely grind the coriander seeds and chillies in a coffee grinder – they do not have to be fine – then add them to the pan and cook for 2 minutes. Stir in the tomatoes, with their juice, paprika, turmeric and water. Bring to the boil, then reduce the heat and simmer, uncovered, for 30–35 minutes.

- Purée the sauce in a blender and return it to the saucepan. Stir in the fenugreek leaves and simmer for 5 minutes. Leave to cool completely. Store in an airtight container in the refrigerator or freezer.

A Guide to Ingredients

Aniseed (*ajowan* or *carum*)
Native to India, aniseeds look similar to celery seeds and are related to caraway and cumin, though the flavour is more akin to thyme. All Indian grocers sell these seeds, which will keep for a number of years if stored in an airtight container. They are used in tiny amounts with fish, with pulses and in fried snacks. Anise aids digestion and helps to prevent wind.

Asafoetida (*hing*)
Obtained from the resinous gum of a tropical plant, asafoetida can be bought from Indian stores in block or powder form. A block is the better purchase as it retains flavour better than the ground spice and will keep well for several months. Asafoetida has a strong flavour and it should be used sparingly.

Bay Leaf (*tej patta*)
Bay leaves used in Indian cooking are obtained from the cassia tree. They are quite different from Western bay leaves, which come from the sweet bay laurel. As Indian bay leaves are rarely available, standard bay leaves have become a popular substitute.

Besan (gram or chick-pea flour)
Made from skinned and ground chick peas, this is available from Indian stores. It has a nutty taste for which there is no substitute.

Black Peppercorns (*kali mirchi*)
Fresh green berries are dried in the sun to obtain black pepper. The green berries come from the pepper vine native to monsoon forests of south-west India. Whole peppercorn keep well in an airtight jar, but ground black pepper loses its wonderful aromatic flavour very quickly. It is best to store whole pepper in a pepper mill and grind it only when required. Pepper is believed to be a good remedy for flatulence.

Cardamom (*elaichi*)
Cardamom has been used in Indian cooking since ancient times. Southern India produces an abundance of cardamom and it is from there that it found its way to Europe along the ancient spice route. There are two types of cardamom, the small green cardamoms (*choti*

elaichi) and the big brown cardamoms, which are also referred to as black cardamoms.

Whole cardamom pods are used to flavour rice and different sauces. Ground cardamom, used in many desserts and drinks, can be bought from most Asian stores. It is best to grind small quantities at home using a coffee mill. Prolonged storage dries out the essential natural oils, which destroys the flavour.

In India, cardamom seeds are chewed after a meal as a mouth freshener. They are often coated in edible silver.

Chapati Flour (*atta*)

This is a very fine wholewheat flour used to make all unleavened Indian breads. It is rich in dietary fibre because, unlike wholemeal flour, *atta* is produced by grinding the whole grain to a very fine powder.

Chillies (*mirchi*)

It is difficult the judge the strength of chillies. Generally, the small thin ones are hot and the large fleshy ones tend to be milder. Most of the heat comes from the seeds, so it is best to remove them if you do not enjoy hot food. One way to do this is to slit the chilli lengthways in half and scrape the seeds away under running water using a small knife. Another way is to hold the chilli between your palms and roll it for a few seconds. This loosens the seeds. Slit the chilli down one side, instead of cutting through completely, and, holding the stem, shake off the seeds.

Always wash your hands thoroughly after handling chillies as their juices are a severe irritant, particularly to the eyes or tender areas of skin. To remove the pungency of the juices, after washing your hands rub a little oil into them, then rub in lemon juice.

FRESH GREEN CHILLIES: Long slim fresh green chillies are sold in Indian stores and by some local greengrocers. Larger supermarkets now sell them, labelled 'finger chillies'. Chillies that come from the Canary Islands tend to be milder than Indian chillies. Jalapeno and serrano chillies from Mexico are more readily available in supermarkets; although these are not ideal for Indian cooking, they can be used.

DRIED RED CHILLIES (*lal mirchi*): When fresh green chillies are ripe, they turn a rich red. These are dried to obtain dried red chillies. Fresh and dried chillies are not interchangeable – when chillies are dried, they change completely. Crushed dried chillies are sold in supermarkets and Indian stores. They can also be prepared at home by crushing

A Guide to Ingredients

dried red chillies in a coffee mill. Dried red chillies are ground into chilli powder.

BIRD'S EYE CHILLIES: These are small, pointed and extremely hot. They are used whole to flavour oil. Long slim chillies are weaker and are ground with other spices.

Cinnamon (*dalchini*)

One of the oldest spices, cinnamon is obtained from the dried bark of a tropical plant related to the laurel family. Its warm flavour is valued in savoury and sweet dishes.

Cloves (*lavang*)

Cloves are dried unripened buds of a South Asian evergreen tree. They have a strong distinctive flavour and are used both whole and ground. In India, cloves are used as a breath freshener. Clove oil is used to ease toothache.

Coconut (*nariyal*)

Coconut palms grow in abundance in southern India and fresh coconut is used in both sweet and savoury dishes. In the West, desiccated coconut, creamed coconut, canned coconut milk and coconut milk powder are convenient alternatives.

Coriander, fresh leaves (*hara dhaniya*)

Widely used in Indian cooking, the fresh herb is used for flavouring as well as garnishing. It is also the key ingredient for many chutneys and pastes.

Coriander, seed (*dhaniya*)

The seed produced by the mature coriander plant is used as a spice. This is one of the most important spices in Indian cooking. Its sweet, mellow flavour blends very well with vegetables.

Cumin (*jeera* or *zeera*)

Cumin seeds can be used whole or ground. Cumin is quite strong in flavour and should be used in measured quantities. Whole seeds are used to flavour oil before cooking vegetables. A more rounded flavour is obtained when the seeds are roasted and ground.

There are two varieties, black (*kala jeera*) and white (*safed jeera*). Each has its own distinct flavour and one cannot be substituted for the other. Black cumin is sometimes confused with caraway.

Curry Leaves (*kari patta*)

Grown extensively in southern India, these have an assertive flavour. They are used to flavour vegetables and pulses. They are sold fresh or dried by Indian shops. Dried leaves can be stored in an airtight jar and the fresh ones, which have a better flavour, can be frozen.

Fennel Seeds (*saunf*)

These green-yellow seeds, slightly larger than cumin, have a taste similar to anise. They have been used in Indian cooking since ancient times. In India, fennel seeds are chewed as a breath freshener or to settle an upset stomach.

Fenugreek, dried (*kasoori methi*)

A strong and aromatic herb, fenugreek is native to the Mediterranean region but cultivated in India and Pakistan. Both the seeds and the leaves (fresh and dried) are used in cooking.

Fenugreek Seeds (*methi dana*)

These tiny, cream-coloured seeds are widely used with vegetables, lentils and some fish dishes. They have a distinctive, powerful flavour and should be used in minute quantities. They are sold in all Indian stores.

Garam Masala

Garam means heat and masala is the blending of different spices. There are many good-quality brands available and the flavour of the bought spice can be enhanced by gently roasting it in a heavy-based pan over low heat for about 1 minute. The main ingredients in this spice blend are cinnamon, cardamom, cloves and black pepper. Other spices are added to these, according to preference. These spices are believed to create body heat and they are used to make spiced tea in extreme climates in the Himalayan region.

Garlic (*lasoon*)

Fresh garlic is indispensable in Indian cooking. Dried flakes, powder and garlic salt cannot create the same authentic flavour. To yield maximum flavour, garlic is always used crushed or puréed. Garlic is believed to be beneficial in reducing the level of cholesterol in the blood and its antiseptic properties aid the digestive system.

Ghee (clarified butter)

Ghee has a rich and distinctive flavour and it is used liberally in Mogul food. There are two types of ghee, pure butter ghee and vegetable ghee. Butter ghee is clarified unsalted butter and vegetable ghee is made from vegetable shortening. Ghee can be heated to a high temperature without burning. Both types of ghee are available from Indian stores and larger supermarkets.

Ghee can be made at home by clarifying unsalted butter. (Vegetable ghee can be made by the same method using margarine made of vegetable oils.) Melt the butter over low heat and allow it to bubble and spatter gently. This is the moisture in the butter and it must be evaporated completely. When the spattering stops, the moisture has evaporated. Continue to heat until the fat is a clear golden colour, with a sediment at the bottom of the pan. The sediment is milk solids. Once the moisture is removed and the milk solids are separated, the ghee is ready. The process can take up to 45 minutes depending on the quantity of butter you are preparing. Cool the fat slightly, then strain it through a sieve lined with fine muslin into a storage container. Ghee does not become rancid, so it does not have to be chilled, but can be stored at room temperature.

Ginger (adrak)

Fresh root ginger is vital to Indian cooking; ground ginger does not give the authentic zesty flavour and warm woody aroma. Dry ginger is, however, used in some dishes, though not in curries. Ginger is believed to improve blood circulation and reduce acidity in the stomach.

Mint (pudina)

Native to Mediterranean and West Asian countries, mint is an essential ingredient in Indian cooking. It is easy to grow and also available in most supermarkets. Dried mint is a good substitute for the fresh herb.

Mustard Seeds (sarsoon or rai)

Mustard seeds are essential in Indian vegetarian cooking. Of the three types available, black and brown mustard seeds are commonly used while white mustard seeds are reserved for making pickles. Black and brown seeds lend a nutty flavour to food. The green leaves are used as a vegetable.

Nutmeg (jaiphal)

Nutmeg has a hard dark brown shell with a lacy covering. This covering is highly aromatic mace (javitri), which is removed from the nutmeg and sold separately. The best way to buy nutmeg is whole. Ground nutmeg quickly loses its lovely aroma and flavour. Special nutmeg graters are available with a compartment to store whole nutmeg.

Onion (pyaz)

Onions are one of the oldest flavouring ingredients; rarely is any savoury Indian cooking performed without them. Brown, red and white onions are grown and used extensively. Shallots and spring onions are also quite common.

Onion Seeds (kalonji)

These tiny black seeds are not produced by the onion plant, but they have acquired this name because they have a striking resemblance to true onion seeds. The seeds are used whole for flavouring vegetables, pickles and Indian breads. These are available in all Indian stores.

Paneer

Often referred to as cottage cheese in India, paneer is quite different from Western cottage cheese. Ricotta is the only cheese that resembles paneer in flavour, but ricotta is softer and does not have the same cooking qualities as paneer. Paneer is a firm, unripened and unsalted cheese that withstands high temperatures to retain its shape perfectly. It is sold in larger supermarkets. The nearest Western cheese in terms of cooking qualities is halloumi, but that is a very salty cheese, so less salt should be added to a recipe when it is used instead of paneer.

Paprika

Hungary and Spain produce mild, sweet peppers that are dried and powdered to make this spice. *Deghi mirchi*, grown extensively in Kashmir, is the main chilli pepper used for making Indian paprika. It is mild and brilliant red in colour, tinting the dishes to which it is added without making them hot.

Poppy Seeds (*khus khus*)

The opium poppy, grown mainly in the tropics, produces the best poppy seeds. There are two varieties, white and black, but only the white seeds are used in Indian recipes. They are usually ground (sometimes roasted) and contribute a nutty flavour to sauces as well as acting as a thickening agent.

Red Lentils (masoor dhal)

These can be bought from Indian grocers or from supermarkets.

Rose Water

This is the diluted essence of a special edible rose, the petals of which are used to decorate Mogul dishes. Rose essence is more concentrated and only a few drops are needed if it is used instead of rose water.

Saffron (*kesar*)

The saffron crocus grows extensively in Kashmir and some 250,000 stamens are needed to produce just 450g (1lb) saffron. It is a highly concentrated spice, used in only minute quantities.

Sesame Seeds (*til*)

These pale creamy seeds have a rich and nutty flavour. They are indigenous to India, which is the largest exporter of sesame oil to the West. Often sprinkled on naan before baking, the seeds are also used with vegetables, to thicken sauces and in some sweet dishes.

Tamarind (*imli*)

Resembling pea pods at first, tamarind pods turn dark brown with a thin hard outer shell when ripe. The chocolate-brown flesh is encased in the shell, with seeds which have to be removed. The flesh is sold dried and it has to be soaked in hot water to yield a pulp. Ready-to-use, concentrated tamarind pulp or juice is quick and easy to use. Valued for its distinctive flavour, tamarind is added to vegetables, lentils, peas and chutneys.

Turmeric (*haldi*)

Fresh turmeric rhizomes resemble root ginger, with a beige-brown skin and bright yellow flesh. Fresh turmeric is dried and ground to produce this essential spice, which should be used in carefully measured quantities to avoid giving dishes a bitter taste.

Yellow Split Peas

These are similar in appearance to channa dhal, but their flavour is not the same. Although they do not have the same nutty flavour, they can be cooked just like channa dhal and are therefore a good substitute. Channa dhal are available in Indian stores.

Yogurt (*dahi*)

In India yogurt is almost always home-made, usually from buffalo milk, which is creamier than cow's milk. Creamy, mild bio yogurt (live yogurt) matches Indian yogurt better then ordinary plain yogurt.

Soups, Starters &
Snacks

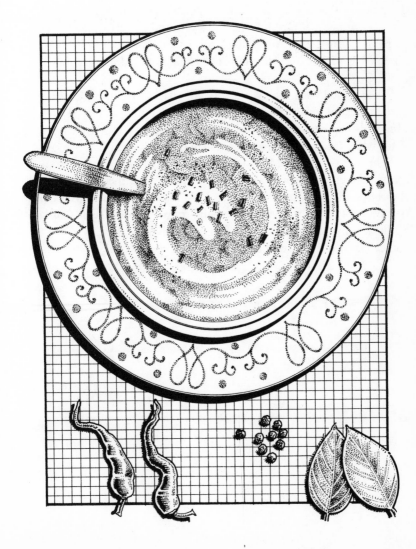

The first course of a meal needs as much planning and imagination as the main attraction. This is the course that creates the first impression, so not only should it taste good, but it must look appetizing. However simple the food, always consider its colour and texture. Plain white plates direct the focus on to the food and show it off to best advantage.

Simple garnishes transform food, bringing instant style to simple dishes. For example, a sprinkling of snipped chives, finely chopped coriander or parsley, or bright rings of red and green chillies make all the difference. Many of the snacks make excellent starters, especially when garnished with fresh fruit. The sweet and tart flavours of fruit perfectly balance spicy foods. Remember that chutneys can be arranged as part of a garnish instead of being offered in a separate bowl.

When served with drinks, many of the snacks look appealing and taste interesting when a little complementary chutney is placed on top. This is also far easier for guests than trying to add a little chutney to a snack while balancing a glass in one hand.

I am sure you will find this chapter a source of inspiration. From formal dinner-party appetizers to irresistible snacks, there is plenty of choice for all occasions. With dishes like Golden Sweet Potato Soup (see page 34) enriched with saffron and soured cream, classic Chicken Mulligatawny (see page 32) and Spicy Squash Slices (see page 46) you can launch every meal in style and with confidence!

TOMATO AND CORIANDER SOUP

Enriched with coconut milk and flavoured with fresh coriander, this superb, lightly spiced soup is quite refreshing. Fresh tomatoes can be used, but bought passata (Italian sieved tomatoes) minimizes both preparation and cooking.

SERVES 4

2 tablespoons sunflower oil or vegetable oil
$\frac{1}{2}$ teaspoon black mustard seeds
$\frac{1}{2}$ teaspoon cumin seeds
1 small garlic clove, crushed
300ml ($\frac{1}{2}$ pint) passata
85g (3oz) creamed coconut, cut into small pieces

2 small green chillies, seeded and chopped
450ml (15fl oz) warm water
2–3 tablespoons roughly chopped fresh coriander leaves and stalks
1$\frac{1}{2}$ teaspoons salt or to taste
1–2 tablespoons sugar
a few fresh mint leaves to garnish

- Heat the oil over medium heat and add the mustard seeds. When they start popping, reduce the heat to low and throw in the cumin seeds followed by the garlic. Fry gently for 15–20 seconds, then add the passata.

- Stir in the creamed coconut, chillies and water. Continue stirring over medium heat until the coconut has dissolved.

- Add the coriander leaves and simmer for 1–2 minutes. Process the soup in a blender or food processor until the coriander and the chillies are finely chopped, then return the soup to the pan.

- Stir in the salt and sugar, then reheat the soup over gentle heat without allowing it to boil. Serve garnished with the mint leaves.

SPINACH AND POTATO SOUP WITH FRESH GINGER

This Goan soup is easy to make and simply delicious. The secret of success lies in starting with a good stock. Supermarkets now sell good-quality fresh stocks which are ideal if you do not have time to make your own. Use chicken stock, or vegetable stock for a vegetarian soup.

SERVES 4-6

30g (1oz) unsalted butter
2–3 shallots, finely chopped
2–3 cloves garlic, crushed
250g (9oz) potatoes, cut into small chunks
115g (4oz) spinach, fresh or frozen, roughly chopped
150ml (5fl oz) water
175ml (6fl oz) single cream
freshly ground black pepper
paprika to garnish

For the stock
600ml (1 pint) chicken or vegetable stock
1 large onion, unpeeled, quartered
3–4 large garlic cloves, unpeeled, bruised
1cm (½in) cube fresh root ginger, unpeeled, sliced
1 teaspoon black peppercorns
1 teaspoon salt or to taste

- First flavour the stock: pour it into a saucepan and add the onion, garlic, ginger, peppercorns and salt. Bring to the boil and reduce the heat slightly. Simmer for 12–15 minutes.

- Meanwhile, melt the butter in a saucepan over low heat, then fry the shallots and garlic for 3–4 minutes. Add the potatoes and spinach.

- Strain the stock into the saucepan with the vegetables and add the water. Bring to the boil, then reduce the heat to low. Cover and cook for 10–12 minutes, until the potatoes are tender. Allow to cool slightly, then purée the soup in a blender or food processor.

- Return the soup to the pan and add most of the cream, reserving about 2 tablespoons for garnishing the soup. Taste the soup and add pepper, with salt if necessary. Reheat the soup over low heat and remove from the hob as soon it begins to bubble gently.

• Ladle the soup into bowls and swirl a little cream on top of each portion. Sprinkle with paprika and serve at once.

CHICKEN MULLIGATAWNY

With a title derived from two south Indian words, *mollaga*, meaning pepper, and *tanni*, meaning water, the original mulligatawny was quite different from this delicious soup. It was vegetarian, very peppery and watery in consistency. The name and soup we know today is Anglo-Indian in origin. This version, with chicken, makes an excellent main course when served with boiled basmati rice.

SERVES 4

2 tablespoons unsalted butter
1 large onion, finely chopped
3 large garlic cloves, crushed, or
  1½ teaspoons Garlic Purée (see page 16)
2.5cm (1in) cube fresh root ginger, peeled and finely grated, or
  1 teaspoon Ginger Purée (see page 16)
½ teaspoon ground turmeric
1–1½ teaspoons cayenne pepper or chilli powder
2 teaspoons black peppercorns, crushed

1 tablespoon Ground Roasted Coriander (see page 13)
4 chicken joints (quarters), skinned and halved
1 teaspoon salt or to taste
450ml (15fl oz) hot water
2 tablespoons tamarind juice or
  1 teaspoon tamarind concentrate
2 teaspoons besan (gram or chick-pea flour)
freshly cooked basmati rice to serve

- Melt the butter over gentle heat. Add the onion, increase the heat to medium and fry for 4–5 minutes or until softened. Then add the garlic and ginger, and continue to fry for 2–3 minutes. Stir in the turmeric, cayenne or chilli powder, crushed peppercorns and coriander. Cook for 30–40 seconds.

- Add the chicken and salt, and pour in the water. Bring to the boil, reduce the heat and cover the pan. Simmer for 25–30 minutes, until the chicken is cooked.

- Add the tamarind juice or tamarind concentrate and stir until dissolved. Blend the besan to a smooth paste with a little water, then stir it into the soup and simmer, stirring, for 2–3 minutes. The soup is not very thick – more like a thin batter in consistency.

- Ladle the soup into bowls and serve, offering a bowl of basmati rice from which diners can take as much or as little as they like.

GOLDEN SWEET POTATO SOUP

Although taken from the opposite ends of the spectrum in terms of delicacy, sweet potato and saffron make a harmonious, as well as exotic, combination in this golden soup.

SERVES 4–5

1 tablespoon butter
2 tablespoons sunflower oil or
    vegetable oil
250g (9oz) leeks, roughly chopped
2 garlic cloves, crushed
1 small green chilli, seeded and
    chopped
1 large sweet potato, about 340g
    (12oz), cut into cubes
½ teaspoon Ground Roasted
    Cumin (see page 13)

2 chicken or vegetable stock cubes
½ teaspoon salt or to taste
1.2 litres (2 pints) hot water
good pinch of saffron strands,
    pounded
300ml (½ pint) single cream
freshly grated nutmeg
freshly ground black pepper
snipped fresh chives to garnish

- Heat the butter and oil together in a saucepan and fry the leeks, garlic and chilli for 3–4 minutes over medium heat.

- Add the sweet potato, cumin, stock cubes and salt. Pour in the water and bring it to the boil, then add the saffron and reduce the heat to low. Cover and cook for 15 minutes or until the vegetables are tender. Cool slightly, then process until smooth in a food processor or blender.

- Return the soup to the pan and add the cream. Season with nutmeg and pepper, then stir well and simmer for a few minutes, until thoroughly reheated. Taste and adjust the seasoning if necessary. Serve garnished with the chives.

PRAWN PURI

Although not a traditional Indian speciality, prawn puri are served as a delicious starter in some Indian restaurants. Puris, puffy deep-fried bread, are time-consuming to make, so here I use mini pitta or naan as a base on which to serve the spiced prawns.

MAKES 4

3 tablespoons sunflower oil or vegetable oil
1 teaspoon Five-Spice Mix (see page 13)
1 red onion, finely chopped
2.5cm (1in) cube fresh root ginger, peeled and chopped, or 2 teaspoons Ginger Purée (see page 16)
2–3 large garlic cloves, crushed, or 1½ teaspoons Garlic Purée (see page 16)

½ teaspoon chilli powder
1 teaspoon Fish and Seafood Spice Blend (see page 15)
2 teaspoons tomato purée
½ teaspoon salt or to taste
400g (14oz) peeled cooked prawns, thawed and drained, if frozen
1 tablespoon lemon juice
2 tablespoons finely chopped fresh coriander leaves
4 mini pitta breads or naan
finely shredded crisp lettuce leaves

- Preheat the grill on a medium setting.

- Heat the oil in a small saucepan over low to medium heat and add the five-spice mix. Let the spices sizzle gently for 35–40 seconds before adding the onion. Fry for 5–6 minutes, then add the ginger and garlic. Fry for a further 1–2 minutes.

- Add the chilli powder and fish and seafood blend. Cook for 1 minute, then add the tomato purée and salt. Stir once and add the prawns, then continue to cook for 2–3 minutes, until the prawns are heated through. Stir in the lemon juice and coriander leaves. Remove from the heat and leave in the pan to keep hot while you heat the breads.

- Moisten the breads under running cold water and grill them until they are dry on top. Turn and grill the second side in the same way. Alternatively, do not moisten the breads, but reheat them in an electric toaster on the lowest setting.

- Pile the spiced prawns on the breads and garnish with shredded lettuce. Serve at once.

PRAWN KOFTAS

Prawn koftas are quick and easy to make and they taste simply divine. The light, golden crust encases delicious, lightly spiced ground prawns. Economical, small prawn are ideal as they are ground, rather than used whole.

MAKES 18

1 large egg
2 large slices white bread, crusts removed
1–2 green chillies, seeded if liked
400g (14oz) peeled cooked prawns, thawed and drained if frozen
2.5cm (1in) cube fresh root ginger, peeled and roughly chopped

2 cloves garlic, roughly chopped
2–3 tablespoons finely chopped fresh coriander leaves
2–3 shallots, finely chopped
¼ teaspoon salt to taste
sunflower oil for deep-frying

• Process the egg, bread and chillies in a food processor until smooth. Add the prawns, ginger and garlic. Process for a few seconds, then transfer the mixture to a bowl.

• Add the coriander, shallots and salt, and mix well until thoroughly combined. Shape a small portion of mixture in the palm of your hand to form a walnut-sized ball, pressing the mixture together gently but firmly so that it binds well. Repeat with the remaining mixture to make 18 koftas.

• Heat the oil for deep-frying to 190°C/375°F or until a cube of day-old bread browns in about 60 seconds. Fry the koftas in batches until golden brown. Drain on absorbent paper. Serve with Apple and Coconut Chutney (see page 173).

TURKEY PAKORAS

These deliciously spicy turkey fritters have a way of disappearing in my kitchen before I even have time to finish frying the entire quantity! They really are very moreish. Serve them on their own or with a chutney, such as Fresh Plum Chutney (see page 172) or Apple and Coconut Chutney (see page 173).

SERVES 4-6

550g (1¼lb) turkey breast fillets, cut into 5cm (2in) cubes
1½ tablespoons lemon juice
1½ teaspoons salt or to taste
1 tablespoon Vegetable and Poultry Spice Blend (see page 14)
115g (4oz) besan (gram or chick-pea flour), sifted

55g (2oz) cornflour
½ teaspoon aniseeds
2 tablespoons chopped fresh coriander leaves
1 egg, beaten
120ml (4fl oz) water
oil for deep-frying

- Place the turkey on a large plate and sprinkle with the lemon juice, half the salt and half the vegetable and poultry spice blend. Mix thoroughly and set aside.

- In a mixing bowl, mix the besan and cornflour together, then stir in the aniseeds and the remaining salt and spice blend. Add the coriander leaves and the egg, then gradually add the water, stirring continuously, to make a smooth batter.

- Heat the oil for deep-frying to 190°C/375°F or until a cube of day-old bread browns in about 45 seconds. Dip each piece of turkey in the spiced batter and add to the hot oil. Do not add more than can be cooked in a single layer. Fry for 4–5 minutes over medium-high heat, until well browned. Drain on absorbent paper and keep hot until all the pakoras are cooked.

Minced Lamb Kababs

Mutton is traditional in these kababs, but lamb or beef are good alternatives. Serve them with Mint and Yogurt Chutney (see page 169) as a snack or wrap them in chapatis or soft wheat-flour tortillas to make a light meal. For a substantial meal, serve them in wholemeal pitta breads with sliced or chopped onions, cucumber, lettuce and chilli sauce or tomato ketchup.

MAKES 12

55g (2oz) unsalted cashew nut pieces

1 large egg

2 tablespoons single cream

1 slice white bread, crusts removed, cut into small pieces

1 small onion, roughly chopped

2 large garlic cloves, roughly chopped

2.5cm (1in) cube fresh root ginger, peeled and roughly chopped

1–3 green chillies, seeded if liked, roughly chopped

2–3 tablespoons roughly chopped fresh coriander leaves

1½ teaspoons Ground Roasted Coriander (see page 13)

1½ teaspoons Ground Roasted Cumin (see page 13)

1 teaspoon salt or to taste

450g (1lb) lean minced lamb

sunflower oil for brushing

- Preheat the grill on the hottest setting. Line a grill pan with foil and brush the foil with a little oil.

- Process the cashew nuts, egg, cream and bread in a food processor until smooth. Add the remaining ingredients and process until fine.

- Divide the mixture into 12 equal portions and shape them into balls, then flatten these into small round cakes, each about 1cm (½in) thick.

- Place the kababs on the prepared grill pan and brush them with oil. Grill about 7.5cm (3in) below the heat source for 4–5 minutes. Turn the kababs and brush the uncooked side with oil. Grill for a further 4–5 minutes. Serve immediately.

KHEEMA NAAN

This is one of the most popular items on restaurant menus. Made by the traditional method, this naan requires lengthy preparation, but this recipe uses bought bread. The fingers of kheema naan are delicious with drinks or as an accompaniment to soup; or serve them with a side salad to make a tasty mid-week meal.

SERVES 8

8 bought plain naan or wholemeal pitta breads
2 large eggs
450g (1lb) minced lamb, pork or beef
2 large garlic cloves, roughly chopped
2.5cm (1in) cube fresh root ginger, roughly chopped

1–3 green chillies, seeded if liked
3–4 tablespoons roughly chopped fresh coriander leaves
2 tablespoons roughly chopped fresh mint leaves
1 teaspoon garam masala
1 small onion, roughly chopped
1 teaspoon salt or to taste
2 tablespoons butter, melted

- Preheat the grill on the hottest setting and line a grill pan with foil. Arrange the naan or pitta breads in the pan.

- Put 1 egg in a food processor and add all the remaining ingredients except the butter. Process the mixture until it is smooth, then divide it into 8 equal portions.

- Beat the remaining egg and brush it generously over the breads. Spread a portion of the mince mixture evenly over each bread, making sure the surface is covered completely. Drizzle the melted butter over the top.

- Grill the breads about 12cm (5in) below the heat source for about 5 minutes, or until the meat topping is thoroughly cooked and browned. Cut the kheema nan across into wide strips and serve hot.

PANEER KABABS STUFFED WITH DRIED PRUNES

These delectable kababs delight vegetarians! If you really want to cut the preparation time to the minimum, use whole prunes, but I prefer to chop them as they are easier to eat, especially when they are part of the menu for a buffet party. Serve a chutney, such as Apple and Coconut (see page 173), and a side salad with the kababs to make a tempting starter.

MAKES 12

30g (1oz) besan (gram or chick-pea flour), sifted
30g (1oz) cornmeal or polenta
½ teaspoon Ground Roasted Cumin (see page 13)
1 teaspoon Ground Roasted Coriander (see page 13)
250g (9oz) paneer or halloumi cheese, grated
1 small onion, grated

1–2 green chillies, seeded if liked, finely chopped
1 tablespoon chopped fresh mint
2 tablespoons chopped fresh coriander leaves
2 tablespoons lemon juice
15–17 ready-to-eat prunes, chopped
2 tablespoons cornflour
oil for deep-frying

- Mix the besan and cornmeal or polenta together in a bowl. Add the remaining ingredients, except the prunes, oil and cornflour, then mix thoroughly. Taste the mixture and add salt only if you are using paneer. (Halloumi can be quite salty.)

- Divide the mixture into 12 equal portions and roll them into balls. Flatten a ball of mixture on the palm of your hand and place a little of the chopped prune in the centre. Shape the mixture around the chopped prune to enclose it completely in a ball. Make sure that the prune stuffing is completely covered, then gently flatten the ball to a cake 1cm (½in) thick. Repeat with the remaining mixture and chopped prunes.

- Heat the oil for deep-frying to 190°C/375°F or until a cube of day-old bread browns in about 45 seconds. Dust each kebab in cornflour and shake off any excess, then add to the oil. Fry as many as you can in a single layer in the pan, allowing 3–4 minutes, or until the kababs are well browned. Drain on kitchen paper and keep hot while frying the remaining kababs.

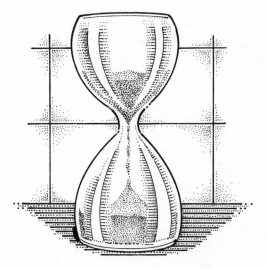

Soups, Starters & Snacks

QUORN KABABS

These kababs make an excellent snack or a vegetarian main meal. They can be served in pitta breads, with a salad or relish, or they make an exciting meal when served with Spiced Potato Wedges (see page 146) and Onion Raita with Roasted Peanuts (see page 177).

MAKES 14

55g (2oz) unsalted cashew nut pieces
1 large slice white bread, crusts removed
1 large egg
2 tablespoons double cream
1cm (1/2in) cube fresh root ginger, peeled and roughly chopped
1 large garlic clove, roughly chopped
1/2–1 teaspoon chilli powder
15g (1/2oz) fresh coriander leaves and stalks, roughly chopped
2 tablespoons roughly chopped fresh mint leaves
1 teaspoon salt or to taste
1 teaspoon garam masala
300g (10 1/2oz) Quorn mince
1 small onion, roughly chopped
sunflower oil for shallow frying

• Process the cashew nuts, bread and egg in a food processor until smooth. Add the remaining ingredients, except the onion and oil, and blend the mixture to a smooth paste. Add the onion and pulse the power until it is finely chopped, but not puréed.

• Divide the mixture into 14 equal portions and shape them into balls. Flatten the balls into small round cakes, about 2.5cm (1in) in diameter.

• Heat about 2.5cm (1in) depth of oil in a frying pan. Fry the kababs until golden brown on both sides. Drain on absorbent paper and serve.

EGG KOFTAS

These may sound like the mini savoury eggs sold in the supermarkets, but in reality they are nothing like them. Full of wonderful flavours, they are great for buffet parties and picnics. They are so quick and easy to make that they are also good as salad or vegetable accompaniments for lunch or dinner.

MAKES 20

1 large slice white bread, crusts removed

115g (4oz) Cheddar cheese, roughly chopped

2–3 tablespoons roughly chopped fresh coriander leaves and stalks

1–2 green chillies, seeded if liked

5mm (¼in) cube fresh root ginger, peeled and chopped

½ teaspoon salt or to taste

1 egg, beaten

3 large hard-boiled eggs

1 heaped tablespoon cornflour

sunflower oil for deep-frying

- Process the bread and cheese in a food processor until reduced to crumbs. Add the chopped coriander, chillies, ginger, salt and beaten egg. Process until the ingredients are well blended, then add the hard-boiled eggs and pulse the power to chop the eggs finely into the mixture.

- Shape the mixture into 20 walnut-sized balls or koftas and dust them in cornflour.

- Heat the oil for deep-frying to 190°C/375°F or until a cube of day-old bread browns in about 45 seconds. Shake any excess cornflour off the koftas as you add them to the oil in batches and fry crisp and golden. Drain on paper.

SWEET POTATO CAKES

These make a tasty snack when served with Rhubarb Chutney with Roasted Cumin (see page 170). For a satisfying main meal add a salad and Broccoli and Red Pepper Raita (see page 174) or Tomato Raita (see page 175).

MAKES 12

2 sweet potatoes, about 550g (1¼lb), coarsely grated
1 onion, finely chopped
1–3 green chillies, seeded if liked, finely chopped
3–4 tablespoons finely chopped fresh coriander leaves and stalks
1¼ teaspoons salt or to taste

1 teaspoon aniseeds
1 teaspoon cumin seeds
115g (4oz) besan (gram or chick-pea flour)
55g (2oz) cornmeal
60–75ml (2–2½fl oz) water
sunflower oil for shallow frying

- Place all the ingredients except the water in a large mixing bowl. Mix thoroughly, then gradually add the water and continue mixing to bind the ingredients.

- Divide the mixture into 12 equal portions, and roll them into balls, then flatten them into cakes 5mm (¼in) thick.

- Heat about 2.5cm (1in) depth of oil in a frying pan. Fry the cakes for 3½–4 minutes on each side, until crisp and golden. Drain on kitchen paper and serve hot.

COURGETTE BHAJIYAS

If you are not normally a fan of courgettes, these delicious bhajiyas may just change your opinion. Mixed with onions and spices, and a batter which is made crisp by adding a little semolina, they are a great treat.

SERVES 4–6

100g (3½oz) besan (gram or chick-pea flour), sifted
55g (2oz) semolina
1 teaspoon salt or to taste
1 teaspoon ground turmeric
1½ teaspoons ground cumin
1½ teaspoons ground coriander

175–200ml (6–7fl oz) water
450g (1lb) courgettes, cut into 5mm (¼in) dice
1 onion, chopped
1–3 green chillies, seeded if liked, finely chopped
oil for deep-frying

- Place the besan in a large bowl. Mix in the semolina, salt, turmeric, cumin and coriander, then gradually beat in the water to make a smooth batter.

- Add the courgettes, onion and chillies and mix until the vegetables are thoroughly coated in batter.

- Heat the oil for deep-frying to 190°C/375°F or until a cube of day-old bread browns in about 45 seconds. Add a heaped tablespoon of the mixture to make a bhajiya, then add as many more as can be cooked in a single layer. Fry for 6–7 minutes, until golden brown, then drain on kitchen paper.

- Continue frying the mixture in batches, keeping the cooked bhajiyas hot until all the mixture is cooked.

COCKTAIL BHAJIYAS
Add small spoonfuls of batter to make bite-sized bhajiyas to serve with drinks. Reduce the frying time by 2–3 minutes.

SPICY SQUASH SLICES

I use butternut squash for these fritters, but acorn squash or half a small pumpkin can be used instead. Lightly coated with spiced cornmeal, then deep-fried until crisp, these taste divine – every mouthful will be an explosion of flavour if you serve Rhubarb Chutney with Roasted Cumin (see page 170) as an accompaniment.

SERVES 4–6

1 butternut squash
1 teaspoon salt or to taste
2 teaspoons crushed dried chillies
   or chilli powder
2 teaspoons ground cumin

$\frac{1}{2}$ teaspoon aniseeds or crushed
   fennel seeds
oil for deep-frying
2 teaspoons cornflour
1$\frac{1}{2}$ tablespoons cornmeal

- Peel, halve and trim the squash. Discard the seeds and cut the flesh into slices 1cm ($\frac{1}{2}$in) thick. Lay the slices on a large plate and sprinkle the salt, chillies or chilli powder, cumin and aniseeds or fennel seeds over. Then mix well to coat all the slices evenly.

- Heat the oil for deep-frying to 190°C/375°F or until a cube of day-old bread browns in about 45 seconds.

- Mix the cornflour and cornmeal together in a bowl. Dust the spiced squash slices individually in this mixture and add to the oil, then fry until crisp and golden. Drain on kitchen paper. Serve immediately.

Fish & Shellfish

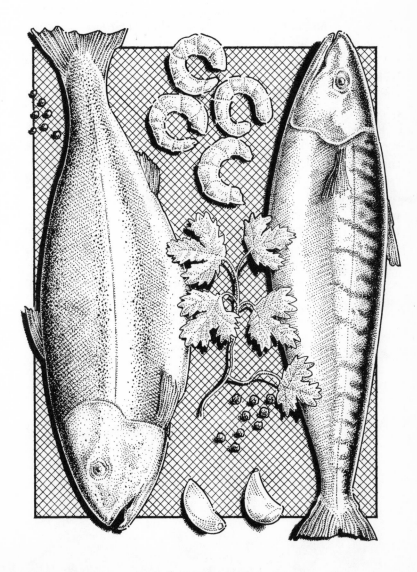

Fabulous spiced fish dishes can be prepared extremely quickly and you will find a variety of dishes to suit all tastes and occasions in this chapter. For example, while sophisticated Tamarind-Coated Trout with Chilli and Tomato Sauce (see page 54) is excellent dinner-party fare, rustic Tuna Burgers (see page 60) are a hit with all the family. In recipes for prawns, I list peeled cooked prawns for speed, but I prefer using uncooked prawns when there is a little time to spare.

With a little imagination plain grilled fish, such as salmon steaks or trout fillets, can be transformed by seasoning (after cooking) with a squeeze of lemon or lime juice and a sprinkling of Ground Roasted Coriander (see page 13) or Ground Roasted Cumin (see page 13). Add a little chilli powder if you like hot food, and some chopped fresh coriander leaves or dill for colour and a fresh flavour. White fish is also good spiced in this way, but it should be moistened with a splash of oil or melted butter before grilling.

Remember that canned fish is a versatile stand-by for mid-week suppers. For a tasty salad, try adding chopped red onions, fresh chillies, chopped coriander leaves and a squeeze of lemon juice to canned tuna or salmon. Moisten the mixture with a little mayonnaise or yogurt to make a super sandwich filling or stuffing for baked potatoes. Canned pilchards are also delicious spiced or added to Bengal Tarka Dhal (see page 124) or Beans and Mushrooms in Chilli Tomato Sauce (see page 126) at the end of cooking and heated through. Serve with boiled basmati rice. When you have sampled the recipes, you will be inspired to prepare all sorts of spicy variations on familiar fish dishes.

COD MASALA

Succulent cod in a moist spice paste is delicious with a plain green salad and sliced red onions sprinkled with lemon juice. Wrap the cod in chapatis or serve with Dill Rice (see page 193) and Bengal Tarka Dhal (see page 124).

SERVES 4

450g (1lb) thick white fish fillets, such as cod, skinned

2.5cm (1in) cube fresh root peeled and ginger, grated, or 2 teaspoons Ginger Purée (see page 16)

4 large garlic cloves, crushed, or 2 teaspoons Garlic Purée (see page 16)

$\frac{1}{2}$–1 teaspoon chilli powder

$\frac{1}{2}$ teaspoon ground turmeric

1 teaspoon paprika

1 teaspoon Ground Roasted Cumin (see page 13)

1 teaspoon Ground Roasted Coriander (see page 13)

1 teaspoon salt or to taste

juice of $\frac{1}{2}$ lemon

2 heaped tablespoons plain flour

2–3 tablespoons sunflower oil

2–3 tablespoons chopped fresh coriander leaves

freshly ground black pepper

- Cut each fillet into 2–3 pieces. Mix the ginger, garlic, chilli powder, turmeric, paprika, cumin, ground coriander and salt. Stir in the lemon juice and 3–4 tablespoons water to make a paste. Set aside. Place the flour on a plate and season it with a little salt and pepper.

- Heat the oil in a frying pan. Dust the pieces of fish in the seasoned flour and fry them in a single layer (in batches if necessary) for about $2\frac{1}{2}$ minutes on each side. Drain on kitchen paper. Return the fish to the pan and remove from the heat.

- Put the spice mixture into a sieve and hold it over the fish, then rub the mixture with the back of a metal spoon to press out all the liquid. Discard the dry spice mixture. Place the pan back over medium heat and stir gently to coat all the fish with spice mixture. Cook until the liquid has evaporated and the spices cling to the fish. Serve at once.

MADRAS FISH CURRY

Firm-fleshed fish is ideal for this dish, but any white fish can be used if the pan is shaken carefully to avoid breaking up the fillets in the sauce.

SERVES 4

2 tablespoons lemon juice
1 teaspoon salt or to taste
675g (1½lb) white fish fillets or
  steaks, skinned and cut into
  7.5cm (3in) pieces
2 tablespoons plain flour
¼ teaspoon chilli powder
½ teaspoon ground turmeric
½ teaspoon fennel seeds, crushed

oil for shallow frying, plus
  1 tablespoon
½ teaspoon black mustard seeds
300ml (½ pint) Madras Curry
  Sauce (see page 17)
8–10 fresh curry leaves or
  1 tablespoon dried curry leaves
2 tablespoons chopped fresh
  coriander leaves

- Sprinkle the lemon juice and ¼ teaspoon of the salt over the fish. Mix the flour, chilli powder, turmeric and fennel together on a plate.

- Heat a little oil in a non-stick frying pan. Dust each of the pieces of fish in the seasoned flour and fry them in a single layer until well browned on both sides. Drain on kitchen paper.

- Heat the 1 tablespoon oil in a large saucepan over medium heat and add the mustard seeds. As soon as they start crackling, add half the madras curry sauce and bring it to the boil. Cook for 2 minutes. Add the remaining sauce and bring it to the boil again, then stir in the curry leaves and the coriander.

- Carefully lay the fish on the sauce. Spoon some of the sauce over the fish and cook gently, uncovered, for 3–4 minutes, shaking the pan from side to side once or twice. Serve with boiled basmati rice and a raita or Carrots in Spicy Split Pea Sauce (see page 155).

COOK'S TIP
The fried fish is also delicious plain, without the sauce. Serve with rice and any vegetable curry or a lentil dish.

FISH PAKORAS

Chunky fillets of haddock or cod are best for this recipe, but you can use any other white fish. To reduce the preparation time, I have cut the fish into larger pieces than usual. In fact, you could leave the fillets whole without increasing the cooking time as it is their thickness that affects the time, not length and width. Spiced Potato Wedges (see page 146) and Tomato Raita (see page 175) or Fresh Plum Chutney (see page 172) are delicious accompaniments.

SERVES 4

4 portions haddock fillet, about 675g (1½lb), skinned
juice of ½ lime
3 tablespoons cornflour
2 tablespoons besan (gram or chick-pea flour)
1 large egg, beaten

1 tablespoon Fish and Seafood Spice Blend (see page 15)
½–1 teaspoon chilli powder
½ teaspoon aniseeds
½ teaspoon salt or to taste
freshly ground black pepper
sunflower oil for deep-frying

• Cut each portion of haddock into 3–4 pieces. Lay the fish in a single layer on a large plate or tray and sprinkle the lime juice over them, then season with salt and pepper.

• Blend the cornflour to a smooth paste with 3 tablespoons water. Add the besan and beaten egg, then mix thoroughly with a fork. Stir in the remaining ingredients except the oil.

• Heat the oil for deep-frying to 190°C/375°F or until a day-old cube of bread browns in about 45 seconds. Dip the fish in the spiced batter until lightly coated, then allow excess to drip off and add to the hot oil. Be sure to shake off excess batter or there will not be enough for all the pieces of fish.

• Fry the fish until crisp and golden. Do this in batches, if necessary, to avoid overcrowding the pan. Drain on kitchen paper and serve.

FISH KORMA

This simply spiced dish is easy to prepare and an impressive choice
for entertaining. The salmon fillets are bathed in a golden sauce
enriched with cashew nuts and aromatic with royal cumin,
cinnamon and cardamom.

SERVES 4

4 salmon fillets, about 675g (1½lb),
  cut into 7.5cm (3in) chunks
2 tablespoons lemon juice
1 teaspoon salt or to taste
4 tablespoons sunflower oil
1 teaspoon royal cumin or caraway
  seeds
2.5cm (1in) piece cinnamon stick

4 green cardamom pods
1 large onion, finely chopped
1–3 green chillies, seeded if liked,
  finely chopped
85g (3oz) roasted cashew nuts
150ml (5fl oz) single cream
1 teaspoon ground turmeric
175 ml (6fl oz) warm water

- Lay the pieces of fish in a single layer on a plate. Drizzle the lemon
juice over them and sprinkle with half the salt, then set aside.

- Heat the oil in a frying pan over gentle heat. Add the royal cumin
or caraway seeds followed by the cinnamon and cardamoms. Fry the
spices gently for about 1 minute.

- Add the onion and chillies and fry over medium heat for 10–12
minutes, stirring regularly, until the onion is pale golden in colour.

- Meanwhile, purée the cashews with the cream, then stir this into the
onions with the turmeric. Pour in the water and add the remaining
salt. Stir well, then lay the fish on the sauce in a single layer. Cover
and cook over low heat for 2–3 minutes.

- Carefully spoon some of the sauce over the fish. Shake the pan
gently and cover it again. Cook for a further 1–2 minutes, then
serve with Saffron Rice (see page 194).

FISH IN AROMATIC YOGURT SAUCE

Fish cooked in yogurt is a firm favourite in Bengal, where mustard oil is used to add a pungent and nutty flavour.

SERVES 4

675g (1½lb) trout fillets, cut into 7.5cm (3in) pieces
juice of ½ lemon
1 teaspoon salt or to taste
250g (9oz) plain yogurt
2 teaspoons besan (gram or chick-pea flour)
½ teaspoon sugar
3 tablespoons sunflower oil
1 teaspoon Five-Spice Mix (see page 13)
2–3 large garlic cloves, crushed, or 1½ teaspoons Garlic Purée (see page 16)

2 bay leaves, crumbled
2.5cm (1in) cube fresh root ginger, peeled and grated, or 2 teaspoons Ginger Purée (see page 16)
1–3 green chillies, seeded if liked, sliced lengthways
½ teaspoon ground turmeric
½–1 teaspoon chilli powder or paprika
2 tablespoons finely chopped fresh dill

• Wash the fish gently and pat it dry with kitchen paper. Pour the lemon juice over the fish and sprinkle with ¼ teaspoon of the salt. Set aside.

• Put the yogurt into a bowl. Add the besan and sugar, then whisk until smooth and set aside.

• Heat the oil in a frying pan large enough to hold the fish in a single layer. When hot, but not smoking (a mustard seed should crackle gently in the oil), add the five-spice mix followed by the garlic, bay leaves and ginger. Fry for 1 minute, then stir in the chillies, turmeric and chilli powder or paprika. Reduce the heat to low and add the whisked yogurt mixture.

• Lay the pieces of fish side by side in a single layer on the spiced yogurt and heat until the yogurt begins to bubble. Cover the pan and cook for 5–6 minutes, adding the dill halfway through. Shake the pan from side to side at least twice during cooking. Serve with boiled basmati rice.

TAMARIND-COATED TROUT WITH CHILLI TOMATO SAUCE

This recipe provides two generous helpings without side dishes or four portions when served with accompaniments, such as Mashed Potato with Mustard-Speckled Coconut Milk (see page 148) or boiled basmati rice and Tarka Channa Dhal (see page 125).

SERVES 2–4

2 large garlic cloves
1 teaspoon salt or to taste
2 tablespoons tamarind juice or
  1 teaspoon tamarind concentrate
$1/2$–1 teaspoon chilli powder
4 large trout fillets
2 tablespoons sunflower oil

1 onion, finely chopped
1–2 green chillies, seeded if liked,
  finely chopped
$1/2$ teaspoon ground turmeric
3–4 small tomatoes, finely chopped
2 tablespoons chopped fresh
  coriander leaves

- Crush the garlic with half the salt, then mix with the tamarind juice and 1 tablespoon water or the tamarind concentrate dissolved in 2 tablespoons boiling water. Stir in the chilli powder. Lay the fish skin side down on a board and rub the tamarind mixture gently over the fillets. Set aside.

- Preheat the grill on a medium setting for 10 minutes and line a grill pan with foil. Grease the foil.

- Meanwhile, make the chilli tomato sauce. Heat the oil in a small saucepan and fry the onion for 6–7 minutes, until pale golden. Add the chillies, turmeric, tomatoes and remaining salt. Reduce the heat to low, cover the pan and cook for 5–6 minutes. Stir in the coriander leaves and remove from the heat.

- Arrange the fish fillets in the prepared grill pan and grill 7.5cm (3in) below the heat source for 5 minutes. Spoon the tomato sauce over the fillets and serve.

RAINBOW TROUT WITH POPPY-SEED SAUCE

Serve these trout on Saffron Rice (see page 194) and offer Tomato Raita (see page 175) or Chunky Tomatoes in Mellow Coconut Sauce (see page 154) as an accompaniment.

SERVES 4

4 small rainbow trout, about 200g (7oz) each, gutted
1 teaspoon salt or to taste
2 tablespoons white poppy seeds
1 tablespoon Ground Roasted Coriander (see page 13)
½ tablespoon ground turmeric
½–1 teaspoon chilli powder
2–3 tablespoons sunflower oil
4 large garlic cloves, crushed, or 2 teaspoons Garlic Purée (see page 16)

2.5cm (1in) cube fresh root ginger, peeled and finely grated, or 2 teaspoons Ginger Purée (see page 16)
1–3 green chillies, seeded if liked, sliced at an angle
15g (½oz) fresh coriander leaves and stalks, finely chopped
150ml (5fl oz) warm water
4 tablespoons single cream
juice of ½ lime

- Preheat the grill to hot and line a grill pan with foil. Grease the foil.

- Make 2–3 deep diagonal cuts on both sides of each trout and gently rub with salt, using ½ teaspoon to season all 4 trout. Place the trout on the prepared pan and grill 7.5cm (3in) below the heat source for 2–3 minutes on each side.

- Grind the poppy seeds in a coffee grinder and transfer to a bowl. Add the ground coriander, turmeric and chilli powder. Stir in a little cold water to make a paste of pouring consistency.

- Heat the oil in a frying pan over low heat. Fry the garlic, ginger and chillies for about 1 minute. Add the spice paste and fry for 3–4 minutes. If the spices stick to the pan, add a little water.

- Stir in the coriander leaves, water, cream and remaining salt. Add the fish and heat until simmering gently, then cook, uncovered, for 2–3 minutes. Carefully turn the fish over and cook for a further 2–3 minutes. Squeeze the lime juice over the fish and serve at once.

SPICED MACKEREL FILLETS

Mackerel are delicious, inexpensive and rich in omega-3 fatty acids which help in the fight against heart disease. Remember to ask the fishmonger to fillet the fish; then this dish can be assembled in minutes. Try Garlic Potatoes with Chilli and Mustard (see page 147) or Mashed Potato with Mustard-Speckled Coconut Milk (see page 148) and a salad as accompaniments.

SERVES 4

4 large or 8 small mackerel fillets
½ teaspoon salt or to taste
juice of ½ lime
1 tablespoon sunflower oil
½ teaspoon Ground Roasted Coriander (see page 13)

½ teaspoon Ground Roasted Cumin (see page 13)
½ teaspoon aniseeds
½–1 teaspoon chilli powder

- Preheat the grill to high. Line a grill pan with foil and grease the foil.

- Lay the mackerel fillets in the prepared pan, skin sides down. Gently rub in the salt and sprinkle the lime juice over the fish. Brush with the oil and grill 7.5cm (3in) below the heat source for 3–4 minutes.

- Mix all the remaining ingredients and sprinkle the mixture over the fish. Grill for about another 1 minute. Serve at once.

SPICED SCRAMBLED EGGS WITH KING PRAWNS

Appearance is just as important as flavour and this striking dish
looks quite glamorous. Creamy golden eggs lightly coat bold king
prawns and the colourful arrangement is accentuated by tomatoes,
coriander leaves and fresh green chillies. Offer naans, pappadums
and Fresh Plum Chutney (see page 172) or bought mango chutney
as accompaniments.

SERVES 4

3–4 tablespoons sunflower oil
½ teaspoon aniseeds
1 red onion, halved and finely
    sliced
1cm (½in) cube fresh root ginger,
    peeled and grated or finely
    chopped, or 1 teaspoon Ginger
    Purée (see page 16)
1–3 green chillies, seeded if liked,
    sliced diagonally
½ teaspoon ground turmeric

1 teaspoon ground coriander
½ teaspoon chilli powder (optional)
400g (14oz) peeled cooked king
    prawns, thawed and drained if
    frozen
½ teaspoon salt or to taste
2 tomatoes, chopped
2–3 tablespoons chopped fresh
    coriander leaves
4–6 eggs, beaten

• Heat the oil in a frying pan over medium heat and add the aniseeds.
  Cook for 10–15 seconds, then add the onion, ginger and green
  chillies. Fry, stirring regularly, for 7–8 minutes, until the onion is
  pale golden in colour.

• Stir in the turmeric, ground coriander and chilli powder (if using).
  Cook for 30–40 seconds. Add the prawns and salt. Stir over
  medium heat for 3–4 minutes. Add the tomatoes and coriander
  leaves, then cook for 2 minutes.

• Pour in the eggs and stir over low heat for 3–4 minutes, until the
  eggs thicken and set to a creamy consistency. Do not overcook the
  eggs or they will be dry. Serve at once.

SPICED PRAWNS WITH FRIED EGGS

This is one of my all-time favourites as a family meal, served with plenty of hot buttered toast triangles. It is also a useful recipe for using up leftover cooked meat, cut into small pieces or minced, instead of the prawns.

SERVES 4

3 tablespoons sunflower oil
1 small onion, finely chopped
1–2 green chillies, seeded if liked, finely chopped
1 teaspoon ground coriander
½ teaspoon mild chilli powder or paprika
400g (14oz) peeled cooked prawns, thawed and drained if frozen

1 tablespoon tomato purée
½ teaspoon salt or to taste
2–3 tablespoons chopped fresh dill or ½ teaspoon dried dill
4 eggs
freshly ground black pepper

- Heat the oil in a frying pan and fry the onion and chilli for 4–5 minutes, until softened.

- Stir in the coriander and chilli powder or paprika and add the prawns. Stir over medium-high heat for 2–3 minutes, then add the tomato purée and salt. Cook for 1–2 minutes, stir in the dill and remove from the heat.

- Fry the eggs, cooking them to taste, then trim the edges of the white using an egg-frying ring, cutter or knife. (You can fry the eggs in egg rings if you have four of them.) Put the spiced prawns in a serving dish, top with the eggs and season with salt and pepper to taste. Serve immediately.

PRAWNS, LENTILS AND GREEN BEANS IN COCONUT MILK

Moong dhal (skinless split mung beans) are traditional for this recipe, but red lentils can be used. Half-fat single cream can be used instead of coconut milk.

SERVES 4

175g (6oz) moong dhal, washed and drained
½ teaspoon ground turmeric
600ml (1 pint) hot water
2 tablespoons sunflower oil or vegetable oil
1 teaspoon coriander seeds
4–6 small dried red chillies (bird's eye chillies) or ½–1 teaspoon crushed dried chillies

¼ teaspoon fenugreek seeds
1 small onion, finely chopped
140g (5oz) fine green beans, cut into 2.5cm (1in) lengths
1¼ teaspoons salt or to taste
200ml (7fl oz) can coconut milk
400g (14oz) peeled cooked prawns
2 tablespoons lemon juice

- Put the moong dhal in a saucepan. Add the turmeric and water, bring it to the boil, then simmer, uncovered, for 10–12 minutes.

- Meanwhile, heat 2 teaspoons of the oil in a small saucepan over low heat. Add the coriander seeds, chillies and fenugreek seeds, and fry gently for 30–40 seconds. Leave to cool, then crush the spices in the oil, in a mortar with a pestle or with the back of wooden spoon to form a paste. Set aside.

- Heat the remaining oil in a frying pan and fry the onion for 7–8 minutes, stirring regularly, until lightly browned. Set aside.

- Add the beans and salt to the dhal and bring back to the boil. Cover and cook over medium heat for 5 minutes. Stir in the coconut milk and prawns, and cook, uncovered, for 5 minutes.

- Finally, stir in the spice paste and onions. Simmer for 1–2 minutes, stir in the lemon juice and serve with boiled basmati rice.

TUNA BURGERS

These are among the best burgers I have sampled. They can be made with any canned fish and are good served in buns, with a little Tomato Raita (see page 175) or plain tomato ketchup and a few crisp lettuce leaves. You can also serve them with Spiced Potato Wedges (see page 146).

MAKES 4

1 tablespoon sunflower oil or vegetable oil, plus extra for frying
1 red onion, finely chopped
1–2 green chillies, seeded if liked, finely chopped
2.5cm (1in) cube fresh root ginger, peeled and grated, or 2 teaspoons Ginger Purée (see page 16)
2 large slices white bread, crusts removed

1 large egg
15g (1/2oz) fresh coriander leaves and stalks, roughly chopped
400g (14oz) can tuna in brine, drained
1 tablespoon cornflour
To serve
4 burger buns
a few iceburg lettuce leaves

- Heat the oil in a small pan and fry the onion, green chillies and ginger for 4–5 minutes. Remove and set aside.

- Process the bread and egg in a food processor or blender until smooth. Add the coriander leaves and tuna, process until smooth and transfer to a bowl. Add the fried ingredients and salt to taste. Divide the mixture into quarters and flatten each portion into burgers 2.5cm (1in) thick.

- Heat enough oil in a frying pan to cover the base to a depth of about 2.5cm (1in). Dust each burger lightly in cornflour before adding it to the pan. Cook over medium-high heat until browned on both sides. Drain on kitchen paper.

- Split the buns and place some lettuce leaves in each, then add the burgers. Serve at once.

SPICED COD'S ROE

This lightly spiced cod's roe makes a rich main course.
Serve it with a bread and relish for a light meal or with
boiled rice and a vegetable curry. It is also delicious with hot
buttered toast – yummy!

SERVES 4

4 tablespoons sunflower oil or
vegetable oil

$\frac{1}{2}$ teaspoon black mustard seeds

1 large red onion, finely chopped

2.5cm (1in) cube fresh root ginger,
peeled and finely grated, or
2 teaspoons Ginger Purée (see
page 16)

1–2 green chillies, seeded if liked,
finely chopped

$\frac{1}{2}$ teaspoon ground turmeric

$\frac{1}{2}$ teaspoon salt or to taste

450g (1lb) fresh or canned cod's
roe

2–3 tablespoons finely chopped
fresh coriander leaves and stalks

- Heat the oil in a non-stick frying pan. When hot, but not smoking,
  add the mustard seeds. As soon as they start popping, add the
  onion, ginger and chillies. Fry, stirring regularly, for 7–8 minutes,
  until the onion is light brown.

- Add the turmeric and salt followed by the cod's roe. Stir-fry for 2–3
  minutes, breaking up the roe. Add the coriander and stir-fry for a
  further 3–4 minutes until the roe is dry and crumbly. Serve at once.

SMOKED MACKEREL ON SPICY VEGETABLE CAKES

Flaked smoked mackerel tossed in lime juice, chilli and coriander enlivens taste buds when served as a topping for delicious savoury cakes.

MAKES 8

200–225g (7–8oz) smoked mackerel fillets, skinned and flaked
1½ tablespoons lime juice
1–2 green chillies, seeded and finely chopped
1 shallot, finely chopped
1 firm tomato, seeded and finely chopped
1 tablespoon finely chopped fresh coriander leaves
For the spicy vegetable cakes
175g (6oz) parsnips, grated

280g (10oz) sweet potato, grated
1 small onion, finely chopped
15g (½oz) fresh coriander leaves and stalks, finely chopped
½–1 teaspoon chilli powder
1 teaspoon salt or to taste
1 teaspoon onion seeds
1 teaspoon aniseeds
85g (3oz) cornmeal
85g (3oz) cornflour
150ml (5fl oz) water
oil for shallow frying

- Place the smoked mackerel in a bowl. Add the lime juice, chillies, shallot, tomato and chopped coriander. Toss lightly and set aside.

- Mix all the ingredients for the spicy cakes in a bowl until thoroughly combined. Divide the mixture into 8 equal portions, then shape these into cakes 1cm (½in) thick. If the cakes feel slightly crumbly, do not worry, they will set quickly when they are added to the hot oil.

- Pour enough oil into a frying pan to cover the base to a depth of about 2.5cm (1in). Heat the oil over medium heat and fry the vegetable cakes in batches, without overcrowding the pan.

- Do not turn the cakes over until you have fried the first side for at least 3 minutes. When browned on both sides, drain the cakes on kitchen paper.

- Arrange the cakes on a serving plate and top with the flaked mackerel. Serve at once.

Chicken & Turkey

Speedy interpretations of classic recipes are balanced by new ideas in this chapter. In many cases I use cook-ahead sauces that you can keep as part of your 'freezer' storecupboard, but you can use shop-bought alternatives. The trick with bought sauces is to add spices to enliven the flavour. For instance, Ground Roasted Cumin and Ground Roasted Coriander (see page 13) with some fresh chillies and chopped fresh coriander leaves or mint lift an anonymous commercial sauce.

The majority of the dishes in this chapter are ideal for freezing. While you are cooking portions for four, double the quantities and freeze half the dish ready for another occasion. Always thaw the frozen food slowly in the refrigerator and heat it thoroughly until piping hot before serving. Add a splash of water to dry or semi-dry dishes before reheating them.

CHICKEN MADRAS

Although chicken (or lamb) madras does not exist as a traditional dish, I have dedicated this recipe to the lovers of meat madras served at many Bangladeshi restaurants in Britain.

SERVES 4

½ teaspoon salt or to taste
1 tablespoon lemon juice
675g (1½lb) boneless chicken breasts or thighs, skinned and cut into 2.5cm (1in) cubes
4 tablespoons sunflower oil or soya oil

1 large onion, finely chopped
300ml (½ pint) Madras Curry Sauce (see page 17)
55g (2oz) creamed coconut, grated or cut into small pieces
½ teaspoon garam masala

- Rub the salt and lemon juice into the pieces of chicken and set aside.

- Heat the oil in a saucepan over low to medium heat. Fry the chopped onion, stirring regularly, for 8–9 minutes, until it is pale golden in colour.

- Add the chicken and stir-fry over medium-high heat for 3–4 minutes, until the pieces change colour and are lightly cooked. Stir in the curry sauce and coconut. Heat until the sauce begins to bubble, then reduce the heat to low and cover the pan. Cook for 15 minutes or until the chicken is cooked through and tender.

- Stir in the garam masala and remove from the heat. Serve with boiled basmati rice or any bread and a raita.

CHICKEN IN GOLDEN CARROT SAUCE

Adding vegetables to meat and poultry dishes avoids having to cook a separate vegetable dish. Serve boiled basmati rice with this chicken dish to make a nutritious, balanced meal; offer grilled or fried pappadums and a simple relish for extra interest.

SERVES 4

1 teaspoon salt or to taste
1 tablespoon lemon juice
675g (1½lb) boneless chicken breasts or thighs, skinned and cut into 2.5cm (1in) cubes
4 tablespoons sunflower oil or vegetable oil
2.5cm (1in) piece cinnamon stick
4 cloves

2 carrots, about 225g (8oz), finely grated
450ml (15fl oz) Northern Curry Sauce or Kadhai Sauce (see page 19)
2 tablespoons double cream
2–3 tablespoons chopped fresh coriander leaves

- Rub the salt and lemon juice into the pieces of chicken and set aside.

- Heat the oil in a wok or frying pan over low heat and add the cinnamon and cloves. Allow the spices to sizzle for 15–20 seconds before adding the carrots. Increase the heat to high and stir-fry the carrots for 3–4 minutes.

- Add 150ml (5fl oz) of the curry sauce and continue to stir-fry for 2 minutes. Repeat this process once more, then add the chicken followed by the remaining 150ml (5fl oz) sauce. Stir once, cover the pan and reduce the heat to low. Cook for 15 minutes or until the chicken is cooked through and tender.

- Stir in the cream and coriander, then remove from the heat. Serve with bread or boiled basmati rice.

FRIED CHILLI CHICKEN WITH COCONUT AND CURRY LEAVES

Fresh curry leaves impart their prominent flavour to this dish. Dried leaves will give a similar flavour if fresh are not available, or coriander leaves can be used for a totally different, but equally delicious, result.

SERVES 4–6

10–12 chicken thighs, skinned
2 tablespoons lime juice
$^1/_2$ teaspoon salt or to taste
240ml (8fl oz) Madras Curry Sauce
(see page 17)

2 tablespoons fresh curry leaves
4–6 green chillies
55g (2oz) creamed coconut, grated

- Rub the chicken thighs all over with the lime juice and salt, then place them in a large sauté pan or fairly deep frying pan and add the curry sauce. Bring to the boil, then reduce the heat to low and cover the pan. Simmer for 20 minutes.

- Remove the lid and increase the heat to medium, then cook for 3–4 minutes. Add the curry leaves and the whole chillies. By this time, the oil used in the sauce and the fat content of the chicken will have seeped out, and the chicken should be frying. Fry over low to medium heat, turning the chicken thighs occasionally to brown them on both sides.

- Finally, add the coconut and continue cooking for 2–3 minutes. Remove from the heat and serve with any bread or rice, such as plain boiled basmati rice or Ginger, Turmeric and Coriander Rice (see page 192), and a raita or vegetable dish.

COOK'S TIP
- Boneless chicken thighs or breast fillets can be used instead of chicken on the bone, in which case reduce the cooking time by about 15 minutes.

CHICKEN IN TOMATO, BLACK PEPPER AND CORIANDER SAUCE

A generous amount of coarsely crushed black pepper gives this chicken curry its characteristic flavour. Combined with lemon juice and tomatoes, the peppery dish is best complemented by boiled basmati rice and, for a contrast in texture, you may like to serve Sweetcorn in Sunflower and Coconut Sauce (see page 151).

SERVES 4

juice of ½ lemon
1¼ teaspoons salt or to taste
4 chicken joints (leg or wing quarters), skinned and chopped into 3 pieces
2.5cm (1in) cube fresh root ginger, peeled and roughly chopped
4–5 large garlic cloves, roughly chopped
2 onions, roughly chopped
4 tablespoons sunflower oil or vegetable oil
5cm (2in) piece cinnamon stick, halved

4 green cardamom pods, bruised
4 cloves
1 teaspoon paprika or mild chilli powder
½ teaspoon ground turmeric
1 tablespoon Ground Roasted Coriander (see page 13)
250g (9oz) canned chopped tomatoes
1 tablespoon black peppercorns, coarsely crushed
240ml (8fl oz) lukewarm water

- Rub the lemon juice and salt into the chicken and set aside. Purée the ginger, garlic and onions in a food processor or blender.

- Heat the oil in a large saucepan and add the cinnamon, cardamoms and cloves. Let the spices sizzle gently until the cardamom pods have plumped up. Then add the puréed ingredients and stir-fry over medium-high heat for 5–6 minutes, until the onion juices begin to evaporate. Reduce the heat to low and continue stir-frying for 3–4 minutes.

- Add the paprika or chilli powder, turmeric, coriander and tomatoes. Cook over medium heat for 5–6 minutes, stirring regularly.

- Add the pepper and arrange the chicken in the pan. Cook over high heat for 4–5 minutes, until the chicken is opaque. Pour in the water and bring to the boil, then reduce the heat, cover and simmer for 25 minutes.

- Remove the lid and cook for 6–8 minutes, until the sauce is reduced to a thick paste. Serve piping hot.

COOK'S TIP
Use a meat cleaver or poultry scissors to cut chicken quarters into smaller portions. Separate the legs from the thighs and cut the thighs into two. If using breast portions, remove the wings and cut the breasts into two.

CHICKEN IN COCONUT AND FRESH CORIANDER CHUTNEY

This taste-bud reviver of a dish can be cooked at supersonic speed compared with many traditional recipes. The green chutney coating the meat looks and tastes appetizing and fresh. Serve chapatis, pitta or naan with Tomato or Radish Raita (see pages 175 and 176) as accompaniments.

SERVES 4

3 tablespoons sunflower oil or vegetable oil

3–4 shallots, finely chopped

1cm (½in) cube fresh root ginger, peeled and grated, or 1 teaspoon Ginger Purée (see page 16)

2 garlic cloves, crushed, or 1 teaspoon Garlic Purée (see page 16)

1–2 green chillies, seeded if liked, finely chopped

675g (1½lb) chicken or turkey thigh fillets, skinned and cut into 1cm (½in) cubes

½ teaspoon ground turmeric

½ teaspoon salt or to taste

½ teaspoon sugar

115g (4oz) plain yogurt, whisked

Coconut and coriander chutney

55g (2oz) desiccated coconut

150ml (5fl oz) boiling water

30g (1oz) roughly chopped fresh coriander leaves and stalks

2.5cm (1in) cube fresh root ginger, peeled and roughly chopped

2 garlic cloves, roughly chopped

1–3 green chillies, seeded if liked, roughly chopped

½ teaspoon salt or to taste

1½ tablespoons lemon juice

- First prepare the coconut and coriander chutney. Put the coconut in a bowl and pour in the boiling water. Leave to soak for 5 minutes. (Use this time to prepare the other ingredients for the chutney.)

- Put the coconut and its soaking water in a blender. Add the coriander, ginger, garlic, chillies, salt and lemon juice. Process until smooth. This will take 5–7 minutes on a medium speed.

- Heat the oil in a non-stick frying pan over medium heat. Fry the shallots, ginger, garlic and chillies for 5–6 minutes. Add the chicken or turkey and stir-fry over medium-high heat for 2–3 minutes, until the meat turns opaque.

- Stir in the turmeric, salt and sugar, and continue stir-frying for 2 minutes. Add 1 tablespoon of the yogurt and cook for 1 minute. Repeat this process twice more, adding half the remaining yogurt each time. Then continue cooking until the yogurt resembles a thick batter and the oil floats on the surface.

- Add the coconut and coriander chutney, and cook for 2–3 minutes, stirring constantly. Remove from the heat and serve at once.

COOK'S TIP
Seed the chillies if you want a mild flavour. Slit them lengthways and use a small knife to scrape out the seeds under cold running water.

DRY-SPICED CHICKEN

There cannot be a speedier Indian recipe for chicken and this can be served in a variety of ways. For a superb light meal, try wrapping the chicken in chapatis, adding chutney or a crunchy salad with finely sliced raw onion. It is also delicious with Mashed Potato with Mustard-Speckled Coconut Milk (see page 148) or with boiled basmati rice and a dhal. The chicken is even good served on its own, as a cocktail snack.

SERVES 4

2 tablespoons sunflower oil or soya oil
4–5 large garlic cloves, crushed, or 2 teaspoons Garlic Purée (see page 16)
675g (1½lb) boneless chicken breasts, skinned and cut into 2.5cm (1in) cubes
1 tablespoon Ground Roasted Coriander (see page 13)
½ teaspoon ground turmeric
½–1 teaspoon chilli powder
1 teaspoon salt or to taste
1½ tablespoons lime juice
2 tablespoons finely chopped fresh coriander leaves

To serve
crisp lettuce leaves, shredded
1 small red onion, finely chopped

- Heat the oil in a large non-stick frying pan over gentle heat. Add the garlic and fry until it is lightly browned. Add the chicken, increase the heat to medium-high and fry for 8–10 minutes, stirring frequently.

- Add the ground roasted coriander, turmeric, chilli powder and salt. Continue cooking for 3–4 minutes, stirring continuously. Stir in the lime juice and coriander leaves, then remove from the heat.

- Arrange the lettuce on one large plate or four individual plates and top with the chicken. Sprinkle with chopped onion and serve at once.

QUICK CHICKEN TIKKA MASALA
This is still the most popular Indian dish. This quick version may not taste exactly like the traditional dish, made with marinated chicken, but it is delicious all the same. Prepare the chicken as above, then stir in

300ml (½ pint) Butter Sauce (see page 18), 2 tablespoons unsalted butter, 120ml (4fl oz) single cream, 1 tablespoon tomato purée and 1 teaspoon sugar. Adjust the seasoning, if necessary, and cover the pan, then simmer the chicken in the sauce for 5 minutes. Serve with Ginger, Turmeric and Coriander Rice (see page 192) or Easy Naan (see page 166).

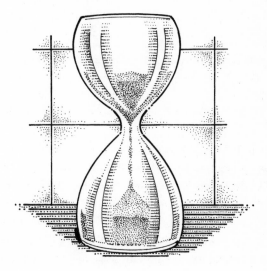

TAMARIND CHICKEN

This low-fat recipe is ideal for everyday eating. Chicken breasts are the best ingredients, but thigh meat can be used. The cooked chicken has very little sauce and is ideal for wrapping up in chapatis. It is also good with boiled basmati rice, accompanied by Bengal Tarka Dhal (see page 124) or Tarka Channa Dhal (see page 125).

SERVES 4

4 boneless chicken breasts, skinned and cut into 5cm (2in) cubes
2½ tablespoons tamarind juice or 2 teaspoons tamarind concentrate
1 teaspoon salt or to taste
1–1½ teaspoons chilli powder
½ teaspoon ground turmeric
150ml (5fl oz) hot water

2 tablespoons sunflower oil or vegetable oil
½ teaspoon black mustard seeds
5 large garlic cloves, crushed, or 2 teaspoons Garlic Purée (see page 16)
1½ teaspoons Ground Roasted Coriander (see page 13)

- Put the chicken, tamarind juice or concentrate, salt, chilli powder, turmeric and water in a saucepan and stir over medium heat until the contents begin to bubble. Reduce the heat slightly and cook, uncovered, for 9–10 minutes, stirring occasionally.

- Heat the oil in a small saucepan. When hot, but not smoking, add the mustard seeds. As soon as the seeds begin to crackle, reduce the heat to low and add the garlic. Fry until the garlic is light brown.

- Pour the fried spices and garlic over the chicken, add the coriander and stir over medium heat for 2–3 minutes, until the sauce has thickened. Serve at once.

CHICKEN MASALA

This is north India's most popular chicken dish, prepared at home and in road-side food stalls, especially in the dhabas, the equivalent of transport cafés.

SERVES 4

2–3 tablespoons sunflower oil or vegetable oil
2.5cm (1in) piece cinnamon stick
4 green cardamom pods, bruised
4 cloves
2 bay leaves, crumpled
4 boneless chicken breasts, skinned and cut into 2.5cm (1in) cubes
1 teaspoon Ground Roasted Coriander (see page 13)
1 teaspoon Ground Roasted Cumin (see page 13)
85g (3oz) plain yogurt, whisked

$^3/_4$ teaspoon salt or to taste
$^1/_2$ teaspoon sugar
300ml ($^1/_2$ pint) Northern Curry Sauce or Kadhai Sauce (see page 19)
2 small tomatoes, chopped
2–3 green chillies, sliced lengthways, or $^1/_2$ green pepper, seeded and cut into julienne strips
$^1/_2$ teaspoon garam masala
2–3 tablespoons chopped fresh coriander leaves

• Heat the oil in a saucepan over low heat and fry the cinnamon, cardamoms, cloves and bay leaves for 20–25 seconds. Add the chicken and stir over medium heat until it turns opaque. Stir in the coriander and cumin and continue to cook for 1–2 minutes. Stir in the yogurt, salt and sugar. Cover and cook for 7–8 minutes, stirring occasionally.

• Heat the curry sauce in a fairly deep frying pan or wok until bubbling. Use a draining spoon to transfer the chicken from its cooking liquid to the sauce. (Reserve the cooking liquid.) Cook, stirring, for 3–4 minutes, then add the tomatoes and cook for 2–3 minutes, until the sauce is thick enough to coat the chicken.

• Pour in the reserved cooking liquid and bring to the boil. Add the chillies or peppers and cook, uncovered, for 2 minutes. Stir in the garam masala and the coriander leaves. Cook for about 1 minute before serving with chapatis or naan.

CHICKEN WITH VEGETABLE MEDLEY

This is one of my favourite chicken dishes and it is a real time-saver. Throw in the vegetables of your choice and the rich, spicy stock will impart a superb depth of flavour to the ingredients. This aromatic dish is full of colour and texture, so I serve it with plain boiled basmati rice.

SERVES 4

85g (3oz) salted cashew nuts, roasted
175ml (6fl oz) boiling water
3 tablespoons sunflower oil or vegetable oil
1 small onion, finely chopped
2.5cm (1in) cube fresh root ginger, peeled and finely grated, or 2 teaspoons Ginger Purée (see page 16)
4–5 large garlic cloves, crushed, or 2 teaspoons Garlic Purée (see page 16)
1 tablespoon Ground Roasted Coriander (see page 13)

1 teaspoon Ground Roasted Cumin (see page 13)
½ teaspoon ground turmeric
½–1 teaspoon chilli powder
8 chicken thighs, skinned
85g (3oz) plain yogurt, whisked
1 teaspoon salt or to taste
1 large carrot, cut into batons (short medium-thick strips)
115g (4oz) fine green beans, cut into 2.5cm (1in) lengths
8 cauliflower florets, each about 2.5cm (1in) in diameter
½ red pepper, seeded and cut into julienne strips

- Place the cashew nuts in a bowl and pour in the boiling water. Set aside to soak.

- Meanwhile, heat the oil in a heavy-based saucepan over medium heat and fry the onion for 5–6 minutes, until it is lightly browned. Add the ginger and garlic and fry for about 1 minute, then reduce the heat to low and add the coriander, cumin, turmeric and chilli powder. Cook for 30–40 seconds.

- Add the chicken and the yogurt. Stir over medium heat until the chicken turns opaque, then stir in the salt. Cover the pan and reduce the heat slightly. Simmer for 20 minutes.

- Meanwhile, purée the cashew nuts with their soaking water in a food processor or blender. Add the purée to the chicken and stir in the carrots and green beans. Bring to the boil, reduce the heat to low and cover the pan. Cook for a further 10–12 minutes.

- Add the cauliflower and cover the pan again. Cook for 5 minutes, until the cauliflower is tender, but still firm. Finally, stir in the pepper strips and simmer, uncovered, for 2–3 minutes before serving.

COOK'S TIP
If you suffer from an allergy to nuts, use 55g (2oz) sunflower seeds or white poppy seeds instead of the cashew nuts in this recipe. To roast either the nuts or the seeds, cook them in a dry, heavy-based pan over low to medium heat until they are lightly browned all over. If you are using roasted sunflower or poppy seeds, you do not have to soak them – simply grind them in a coffee or spice mill until fine and add to the chicken along with 175ml (6fl oz) warm water.

CHICKEN KORMA WITH WHOLE SPICES

I love this korma: it is rich without being fussy, delicious, satisfying and uncomplicated. Offer naan, chapatis or Saffron Rice (see page 194) with the korma.

SERVES 4

55g (2oz) blanched almonds
150ml (5fl oz) boiling water
3 tablespoons sunflower oil or vegetable oil
5cm (2in) piece cinnamon stick
6 green cardamom pods, bruised
4 cloves
2 bay leaves, crumpled
1 small onion, finely chopped
2.5cm (1in) cube fresh root ginger, peeled and grated, or 2 teaspoons Ginger Purée (see page 16)
4 large garlic cloves, crushed, or 2 teaspoons Garlic Purée (see page 16)

1 teaspoon black peppercorns, bruised
½ teaspoon ground turmeric
1 teaspoon mild chilli powder or paprika
675g (1½lb) boneless chicken breasts or thighs, skinned and cut into 2.5cm (1in) cubes
85g (3oz) plain yogurt, whisked
1 teaspoon salt or to taste
2–3 small tomatoes, skinned and chopped
2–3 tablespoons chopped fresh coriander leaves

- Soak the almonds in the boiling water for 10–15 minutes.

- Meanwhile, heat the oil in a heavy-based saucepan over gentle heat and fry the cinnamon, cardamoms, cloves and bay leaves for 30–40 seconds, until the cardamom pods are puffed up. Add the onion and fry over medium heat for 5–6 minutes, until it is pale golden in colour.

- Stir in the ginger and garlic and fry for 1 minute, then add the peppercorns, turmeric and chilli powder or paprika. Stir, then add the chicken and cook, stirring regularly, for 4–5 minutes, until it turns opaque.

- Add the yogurt, salt and tomatoes. Stir until well mixed, then cover the pan and cook over gentle heat for 10–12 minutes.

- Meanwhile, purée the almonds with their soaking water in a food processor or blender. Pour the purée into the chicken, stir well and cover the pan. Simmer for a further 10–12 minutes.

- Stir in the coriander leaves and remove the pan from the heat. Serve at once.

COOK'S TIP

The puréed nuts enrich the sauce, but white poppy seeds or sunflower seeds can be used instead. Use 2 tablespoons poppy seeds or 1½ tablespoons sunflower seeds. There is no need to soak poppy or sunflower seeds, simply grind them in a coffee grinder and fry them with the ginger and garlic. Add 150ml (5fl oz) warm water with the chicken.

MINCED CHICKEN AND VEGETABLE BHUNA

You can use minced chicken or turkey for this super-quick and delicious dish. Serve a bread and chutney or pickle from the storecupboard as accompaniments.

SERVES 4

2 tablespoons sunflower oil or soya oil
30g (1oz) butter
$\frac{1}{2}$ teaspoon cumin seeds
$\frac{1}{2}$ teaspoon onion seeds
450g (1lb) potatoes, cut into small cubes
450g (1lb) minced chicken
450ml (15fl oz) Northern Curry Sauce or Kadhai Sauce (see page 19)

1 teaspoon salt or to taste
115g (4oz) frozen peas
115g (4oz) canned chopped tomatoes
2–3 whole green chillies
2–3 tablespoons chopped fresh coriander leaves
$\frac{1}{2}$ teaspoon garam masala

- Heat the oil and butter together in a non-stick frying pan over low heat. Add the cumin and onion seeds and let them sizzle for 15–20 seconds, then add the potatoes. Increase the heat to medium-high and stir-fry for 5–6 minutes, until the potatoes are lightly browned.

- Add the minced chicken and continue to stir-fry for 8–10 minutes or until the mince is dry and lightly browned. Pour in the curry sauce and add the salt. Stir once, reduce the heat to low and cover the pan. Cook for 8–10 minutes.

- Add the peas and continue to cook for 5 minutes. Then stir in the tomatoes, chillies, coriander leaves and garam masala. Simmer for a final 1–2 minutes before serving.

CHICKEN CUTLETS

Various kinds of cutlets were introduced to Indian cooking during the British Raj, particularly in the east and north-east of India, where they remain popular as a snack to this day. As a young girl, I was always disappointed by the cutlets we ate in restaurants in Calcutta because my mother made the best cutlets. Serve these as a starter or main course.

SERVES 4–8

4 large boneless chicken breasts, skinned
1 tablespoon plain yogurt
2 tablespoons lemon juice
1 onion, coarsely chopped
5cm (2in) cube fresh root ginger, peeled and coarsely chopped
3 garlic cloves, coarsely chopped
1–3 green chillies, seeded if liked, coarsely chopped

½–1 teaspoon chilli powder
1 teaspoon salt or to taste
2 tablespoons chopped fresh coriander leaves and stalks
sunflower oil for deep-frying
For the coating
85g (3oz) plain flour
3 eggs, beaten
115g (4oz) golden breadcrumbs

- Slice each chicken breast in half lengthways so that you have two identical pieces. Put them in a plastic bag, one at a time, and flatten with a meat mallet. Lay them side by side on a large plate.

- Purée the remaining ingredients in a food processor or blender and spread this mixture on both sides of the chicken.

- Heat the oil for deep-frying to 190°C/375°F or until a cube of day-old bread browns in about 45 seconds.

- To coat the chicken breasts, dip them first in flour, then in the beaten egg and finally roll them in the breadcrumbs. Fry the cutlets in a single layer until evenly browned. Drain on kitchen paper and serve freshly cooked.

CHICKEN JHAL FRAZIE

The popular *Jhal Frazie* was created during the days of the British Raj as a dish for using up cold cooked meat, particularly the leftovers from a Sunday roast. This recipe comes from Calcutta, where it was served to members of the East India Company.

SERVES 4

8 chicken thighs, skinned
1/2 teaspoon ground turmeric
1 teaspoon salt or to taste
1/2 teaspoon crushed dried chillies or 2 dried red chillies, snipped into pieces
300ml (1/2 pint) water
4–5 tablespoons sunflower oil or soya oil
1 large onion, halved and finely sliced
3 potatoes, about 340g (12oz), cut into small cubes

2.5cm (1in) cube fresh root ginger, peeled and grated, or 2 teaspoons Ginger Purée (see page 16)
3–4 garlic cloves, crushed, or 2 teaspoons Garlic Purée (see page 16)
2 teaspoons Vegetable and Poultry Spice Blend (see page 14)
4 whole green chillies
3–4 small tomatoes, chopped
2–3 tablespoons chopped fresh coriander leaves

- Put the chicken, turmeric, salt and red chillies into a saucepan and add the water. Bring to the boil, cover and cook over medium heat for 15 minutes. Remove the chicken from the stock and allow to cool. Strain and measure the stock – you should have 200ml (7fl oz); if not, add water to make up this quantity.

- Meanwhile, heat the oil in a saucepan and fry the onion over medium heat for 12–14 minutes, until well browned. Use a draining spoon to lift the onion from the pan, and with the back of another spoon press out excess oil, letting it run back into the pan.

- Add the potatoes to the oil remaining in the pan and fry them for 6–8 minutes, stirring regularly, until browned. Add half the reserved stock and cook until the liquid evaporates and the potatoes are tender. Use a draining spoon to remove the potatoes from the pan and drain them on kitchen paper, then set aside in a covered dish to keep hot. Reserve the oil in the pan.

- Meanwhile, remove the meat from each chicken thigh and cut or divide it into quarters, discarding the bones.

- Reheat the oil left in the pan over low heat and fry the ginger and garlic for 1 minute, then add the vegetable and poultry spice blend. Cook for 1 minute. Add the cooked chicken and the remaining stock and cook for 5–6 minutes over medium heat, stirring regularly.

- Finally, add the green chillies, tomatoes and coriander leaves and stir for 1–2 minutes. Transfer the chicken to a serving plate. Arrange the fried potatoes and onions on top and serve at once.

Chicken & Turkey

POUSSINS WITH POPPY SEEDS AND PINE NUTS

Very little oil is used in this recipe, so a non-stick pan is essential.
Saffron Rice (see page 194) and a vegetable dish or a raita
complement the poussins to make a special meal.

SERVES 4

2 poussins
115g (4oz) plain yogurt, whisked
2.5cm (1in) cube fresh root ginger,
   peeled and grated, or 2 teaspoons
   Ginger Purée (see page 16)
4–5 garlic cloves, crushed, or
   2 teaspoons Garlic Purée (see
   page 16)
1 large onion, finely chopped
½–1 teaspoon chilli powder
½ teaspoon ground turmeric
6 green cardamom pods, bruised
1 teaspoon salt or to taste
1 tablespoon pine nuts

2 tablespoons white poppy seeds
2 tablespoons sunflower oil or
   vegetable oil
1 tablespoon Ground Roasted
   Coriander (see page 13)
1½ teaspoons Ground Roasted
   Cumin (see page 13)
150ml (5fl oz) warm water
15g (½oz) fresh coriander leaves
   and stalks, finely chopped
1 tablespoon chopped fresh mint
   leaves
2–3 small green chillies, slit
   lengthways

- Skin the birds first. It is easier if you hold the bird on its back with
  one hand, then use a cloth to pull away the skin. (The cloth
  prevents the fingers from slipping.) Cut off and discard the leg and
  wing tips. Halve the birds down the middle of the breastbone, then
  joint them, so that the wings are attached to the breasts and the legs
  and thighs are joined. You do not need the bony backs for this dish,
  but they can be used to make stock.

- Put the poussin joints in a large non-stick sauté pan or frying pan
  with a lid. Add the yogurt, ginger, garlic, onion, chilli powder,
  turmeric, cardamom pods and salt. Stir over medium heat for 4–5
  minutes, until the joints are opaque. Cover and reduce the heat to
  low. Cook for 15 minutes, stirring once or twice. Remove the lid
  and cook, uncovered, over medium-high heat until the sauce
  resembles a very thick batter.

- Meanwhile, grind the pine nuts in a coffee mill or spice mill until they are finely chopped. Add the poppy seeds and grind until fine.

- Add the oil, ground coriander and cumin to the cooked poussins and stir over medium heat for 2–3 minutes. Add the ground pine-nut mixture and reduce the heat to low. Continue to fry for 5–6 minutes, stirring regularly, until the poussins begin to brown.

- Pour in the water and continue to cook for 2–3 minutes. Add the chopped coriander, mint and chillies. Cook for 1–2 minutes, then serve.

CHICKEN PILAU

Using chicken thighs on the bone gives this pilau additional flavour, but boneless chicken meat will also give a perfectly acceptable result.

SERVES 4

280g (10oz) basmati rice
2 tablespoons ghee or unsalted butter
1 large onion, halved and finely sliced
2.5cm (1in) cube fresh root ginger, peeled and grated, or 2 teaspoons Ginger Purée (see page 16)
3–4 large garlic cloves, crushed, or 2 teaspoons Garlic Purée (see page 16)
1½ tablespoons Vegetable and Poultry Spice Blend (see page 14)

8 chicken thighs, skinned and halved
2 teaspoons salt or to taste
115g (4oz) plain yogurt, whisked
600ml (1 pint) hot water
6 green cardamom pods, bruised
2 bay leaves, crumbled
6 cloves
5cm (2in) piece cinnamon stick, halved
10–12 black peppercorns
To garnish
toasted flaked almonds
sprigs of fresh coriander

- Wash the rice and soak it in cold water for 15 minutes.

- Meanwhile, melt the ghee or butter in a saucepan and fry the onion for 10–12 minutes, stirring regularly, until lightly browned.

- Add the ginger and garlic, and cook for 2–3 minutes, then add the vegetable and poultry spice blend. Cook for a further 2–3 minutes. Add the chicken with 1 teaspoon of the salt and cook, stirring frequently, for 3–4 minutes, until the chicken is opaque.

- Pour in the yogurt and stir over low heat. Cover and cook for 20 minutes. Remove the lid and stir-fry the chicken over medium heat for 4–5 minutes, until the sauce resembles a thick batter. Remove from the heat and set aside.

- Bring the hot water to the boil in a saucepan large enough to hold the chicken and the rice together. Drain the rice and add it to the water with the cardamoms, bay leaves, cloves, cinnamon and peppercorns.

- Add the reserved salt and bring the water back to the boil. Reduce the heat to medium and cook, uncovered, until the surface water has evaporated. Then reduce the heat to very low and cook for 2–3 minutes.

- Spoon the chicken and its sauce over the rice, cover and cook over very low heat (use a heat diffuser if necessary) for 5 minutes. Remove from the heat and leave to stand for 6–8 minutes. Transfer to a serving dish and garnish with the almonds and coriander.

CHICKEN PASANDA

Pasanda is the term for thin strips of meat (similar to goujons).
Use a batch of prepared Butter Sauce (see page 18) to make this
delicious *pasanda* with speed and ease.

SERVES 4

4 boneless chicken breasts, skinned
4 tablespoons sunflower oil or
vegetable oil
4 green cardamom pods
2.5cm (1in) piece cinnamon stick
3–4 shallots, finely chopped
1½ teaspoons Vegetable and Poultry
Spice Blend (see page 14)

115g (4oz) plain yogurt
150ml (5fl oz) Butter Sauce (see
page 18)
½ teaspoon salt or to taste
2 green chillies
½ teaspoon garam masala
2–3 tablespoons chopped fresh
coriander leaves

- Cut the chicken breasts into thin strips, about 5mm (¼in) thick and 5cm (2in) long.

- Heat the oil in a saucepan over low heat. Fry the cardamoms and cinnamon until the cardamom pods are puffed up, then add the shallots. Fry for 8–10 minutes, stirring regularly, until the shallots are lightly browned.

- Add the vegetable and poultry spice blend and sauté for 1 minute, then add the chicken. Stir over medium heat for 4–5 minutes, until opaque.

- Whisk the yogurt and add it to the chicken, then cook for 2–3 minutes before adding the butter sauce and salt. Stir, reduce the heat to low and cover the pan. Cook for 10 minutes.

- Slit the chillies lengthways into halves or quarters according to their size. Remove and discard their seeds if you like, then add the chillies to the chicken. Add the garam masala and coriander leaves and cook, uncovered, for 2–3 minutes. Remove from the heat and serve with Saffron Rice (see page 194).

COOK'S TIP
Whisking yogurt before adding it to a dish helps to prevent it from curdling during cooking.

MASALA CHICKEN LIVERS

Chicken livers are inexpensive, quick to cook and delicious with a little spice. Serve chapatis, soft tortillas or wholemeal pitta bread and a salad with this dish. It is also delicious with Ginger, Turmeric and Coriander Rice (see page 192) and a raita.

SERVES 4

4–5 tablespoons sunflower oil or vegetable oil
1 large onion, halved and finely sliced
675g (1½lb) chicken livers, trimmed
1½ tablespoons plain flour
1 teaspoon salt or to taste
1 teaspoon ground cumin

1 teaspoon garam masala
½–1 teaspoon chilli powder
4 large garlic cloves, crushed, or 2 teaspoons Garlic Purée (see page 16)
2 small tomatoes, chopped
2–3 tablespoons chopped fresh coriander leaves

- Heat the oil in a large non-stick frying pan and fry the onion for 12–15 minutes, stirring regularly, until well browned.

- Meanwhile, spread out the livers on a large plate. Mix the flour with the salt, cumin, garam masala and chilli powder and sprinkle this mixture over the liver. Sprinkle 1 tablespoon water over and mix well.

- Use a draining spoon to remove the onions from the pan, pressing out the excess oil with the back of a smaller spoon and letting it drain into the pan. Drain the onions on kitchen paper and set aside.

- Fry the garlic in the remaining oil for 2–3 minutes. Add half the liver and fry until it changes colour, then add the rest of the liver and fry for a further 3–4 minutes. (Reserve any remaining seasoned flour from the liver.) Reduce the heat to low.

- Mix 2–3 tablespoons water with the leftover flour and add this to the pan. Simmer for 2–3 minutes, then stir in the tomatoes and coriander leaves. Serve at once, garnished with the fried onions.

TURKEY SIMMERED IN MASALA DHAL

Red lentils can be used instead of the moong dhal, but avoid whole green or brown lentils that require longer cooking as you really do need quick-cooking lentils for this recipe.

SERVES 4

3 tablespoons sunflower oil or vegetable oil

7.5cm (3in) piece cinnamon stick, halved

6 cloves

1 large onion, finely chopped

2.5cm (1in) cube fresh root ginger, peeled and finely grated, or 2 teaspoons Ginger Purée (see page 16)

4–5 large garlic cloves, crushed, or 1 tablespoon Garlic Purée (see page 16)

1 tablespoon Vegetable and Poultry Spice Blend (see page 14)

1 teaspoon Meat and Pulses Spice Blend (see page 15)

450g (1lb) turkey thigh fillets or leg steaks, cut into 5mm (¼in) dice

2 tablespoons plain yogurt, whisked

2 teaspoons tomato purée

225g (8oz) moong dhal (skinless split mung beans), washed and soaked for 15 minutes

1¼ teaspoons salt or to taste

600ml (1 pint) lukewarm water

1 medium tomato, chopped

2–3 whole green chillies

2–3 tablespoons finely chopped fresh coriander leaves and stalks

- Heat the oil in a frying pan over low heat and fry the cinnamon and cloves for 25–30 seconds. Add the onion and fry over medium heat, stirring regularly, for 6–7 minutes, until lightly browned. Add the ginger and garlic and fry for 1 minute.

- Stir in both the spice blends and cook for 1 minute, then add the turkey. Stir-fry over high heat for 2–3 minutes, until the turkey is opaque. Add half the yogurt and stir-fry for 2 minutes, then add the remaining yogurt and stir-fry for a further 2 minutes. Reduce the heat to low, cover and simmer for 10 minutes.

- Add the tomato purée and stir-fry for 1–2 minutes, then add the moong dhal and salt. Continue to stir-fry for 2 minutes. Pour in

150ml (5fl oz) of the water and cook until it evaporates before pouring in the remaining water. Stir in the tomato and bring to the boil. Cover and cook over low heat for 20 minutes, stirring halfway through cooking.

- Finally, stir in the chillies and coriander leaves, and cook for 2 minutes. Serve with boiled basmati rice and a raita.

BREAST OF TURKEY IN SOURED CREAM AND CORIANDER SAUCE

Both chicken and turkey work well in this recipe which is impressive, yet easy to cook. Easy Naan (see page 166) or Saffron Rice (see page 194) is a suitable accompaniment.

SERVES 6

3 tablespoons sunflower oil or vegetable oil

5cm (2in) cube fresh root ginger, peeled and grated, or 1 tablespoon Ginger Purée (see page 16)

6 large garlic cloves, crushed, or 1 tablespoon Garlic Purée (see page 16)

2.5cm (1in) piece cinnamon stick

6 green cardamom pods, bruised

2 tablespoons Vegetable and Poultry Spice Blend (see page 14)

1 teaspoon paprika

260ml (9fl oz) warm water

2 tablespoons ground almonds

1kg (2¼lb) turkey breast fillets, skinned and cut into 5cm (2in) cubes

115g (4oz) plain yogurt, whisked

good pinch of saffron strands, pounded

30g (1oz) chopped coriander leaves and stalks

2–4 green chillies, seeded if liked, slit lengthways

400g (14oz) potatoes, cut into 5cm (2in) cubes

1½ teaspoons salt or to taste

150ml (5fl oz) soured cream

- Heat the oil in a large saucepan over low heat and add the ginger, garlic, cinnamon and cardamoms. Fry gently for 1–2 minutes. Add the vegetable and poultry spice blend and paprika. Cook for 1 minute, then pour in 60ml (2fl oz) of the water. Cook for 2–3 minutes, stirring, until the water evaporates.

- Stir in the ground almonds and cook for 1 minute, then add the turkey, whisked yogurt and saffron. Cook over medium heat for 2–3 minutes before adding the coriander leaves, chillies, potatoes and salt. Bring to a gentle simmer, cover and cook for 25 minutes or until the turkey and potatoes are cooked through and tender.

- Beat the soured cream with a fork and stir it into the curry. Cook over low heat, uncovered, for 7–8 minutes, then serve.

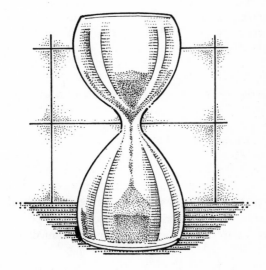

TURKEY BHUNA

As *bhuna* (stir-fried) dishes are fairly dry, they are served with
either unleavened bread, such as chapatis, or rice and dhals. For the
first 25 minutes the meat needs little attention and this is ample
time in which to cook a lentil dish, such as Bengal Tarka Dhal (see
page 124) or Tarka Channa Dhal (see page 125). Cook the rice to
go with the meal in the microwave, where it requires absolutely
no attention.

SERVES 4

675g (1½lb) boneless turkey thighs
or breasts, skinned and cut into
2.5cm (1in) cubes

115g (4oz) plain yogurt, whisked

5cm (2in) cube fresh root ginger,
peeled and finely grated, or
1 tablespoon Ginger Purée (see
page 16)

5–6 large garlic cloves, crushed, or
1 tablespoon Garlic Purée (see
page 16)

1 teaspoon Ground Roasted Cumin
(see page 13)

1 teaspoon Ground Roasted
Coriander (see page 13)

½ teaspoon ground turmeric

1–1½ teaspoons chilli powder

1 teaspoon salt or to taste

55g (2oz) ghee or unsalted butter

90ml (3fl oz) warm water

2–3 tablespoons chopped fresh
coriander leaves

½ teaspoon garam masala

- Put the turkey into a heavy-based saucepan. Add the yogurt, ginger,
  garlic, cumin, ground coriander, turmeric, chilli powder and salt.
  Bring slowly to simmering point over low to medium heat. Cover
  and simmer for 20–25 minutes.

- Remove the lid and cook the chicken for 6–7 minutes, until
  completely dry. Add the butter and cook over medium heat, stirring
  almost continuously, for 5–6 minutes, until the chicken has
  browned.

- Stir in the warm water and continue to cook for 2–3 minutes over
  low heat. Finally, add the coriander leaves and garam masala, stir for
  1 minute and remove from the heat. Serve at once.

Lamb & Pork

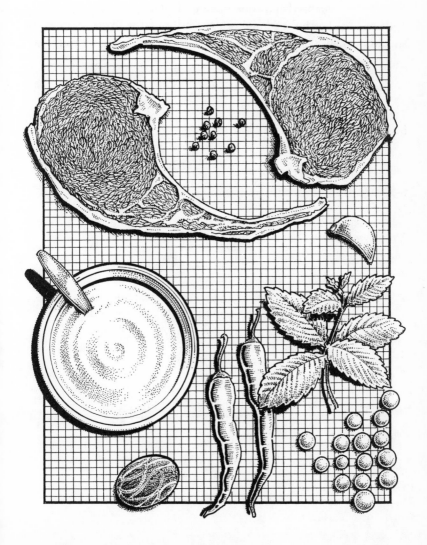

Indian recipes for lamb and pork are usually based on long, slow cooking methods rather than speedy grilling, allowing the flavours of the spices to penetrate deep into the meat. Meat is always well cooked; there are no rare or briefly cooked dishes, leaving meat pink in the middle. For this reason, I have based the recipes in this chapter on quick-cooking cuts and types of meat, such as mince, liver, sausages and bacon. The exception is a recipe for lamb cutlets, which are briefly marinated and pan-fried.

The majority of these dishes can be frozen, so take the opportunity to be super-organized and cook them in double quantities, then set aside half the batch for future meals. As always, the frozen dishes should be thawed slowly in the refrigerator before being thoroughly reheated until piping hot.

FRIED PORK WITH DILL AND CHILLIES

This is an Anglo-Indian recipe from Calcutta. Authentically, fatty pork is used, but I prefer leaner pork loin steaks for quick cooking and they are superb with dill, which has a particular affinity for pork. Any bread or boiled basmati rice and a vegetable or lentil dish will complement the pork.

SERVES 4

3–4 tablespoons sunflower oil
675g (1½lb) pork loin steaks, trimmed and cut into 1 x 2.5cm (½ x 1in) strips
5cm (2in) cube fresh root ginger, peeled and grated, or 1½ tablespoons Ginger Purée (see page 16)
1 teaspoon ground turmeric
1 large onion, halved and finely sliced

½–1 teaspoon chilli powder
2 teaspoons Ground Roasted Coriander (see page 13)
1 teaspoon salt or to taste
60ml (2fl oz) white wine vinegar
120ml (4fl oz) warm water
1–3 green chillies, seeded if liked, sliced at a slant
3–4 tablespoons chopped fresh dill

- Heat the oil in a frying pan over medium heat until smoking hot. Add the pork and stir over medium-high heat for 4–5 minutes.

- Add the ginger, turmeric and onion. Continue frying for 4–5 minutes. Stir in the chilli powder, coriander and salt, and fry for a further 3–4 minutes.

- Pour in the vinegar and half the water, then continue to cook, stirring, for 4–5 minutes. Pour in the remaining water and cook over medium heat for 4–5 minutes, stirring regularly.

- Add the chillies and dill, then cook for 2–3 minutes. The cooked pork should be coated with the spices, chillies and dill. Serve at once.

PAN-FRIED LAMB CUTLETS WITH SPICY GREEN PEA SAUCE

Marinate the lamb in the refrigerator for 2–3 hours, or even overnight, if possible; if you cannot spare this much time, start by marinating them before you make the sauce and any other dishes you plan to serve. Chapatis, naan or boiled basmati rice, and a salad or raita, are suitable accompaniments.

SERVES 4

8 lamb cutlets
85g (3oz) plain yogurt, whisked
2.5cm (1in) cube fresh root ginger, peeled and finely grated, or 2 teaspoons Ginger Purée (see page 16)
4 large garlic cloves, crushed, or 2 teaspoons Garlic Purée (see page 16)
½ teaspoon ground turmeric

½ teaspoon grated nutmeg
1 teaspoon salt or to taste
4 tablespoons sunflower oil
1 teaspoon cumin seeds
1–3 dried red chillies, chopped
225g (8oz) frozen peas
350ml (11fl oz) warm water
1 tablespoon chopped fresh mint leaves or ½ teaspoon dried mint
2 tomatoes, skinned and chopped

- Put the cutlets in a non-metallic bowl. Mix the yogurt, ginger, garlic, turmeric, nutmeg and ½ teaspoon of the salt, then pour this over the lamb cutlets. Rub the yogurt mixture into the meat and set aside to marinate.

- Heat half the oil in a saucepan over medium heat. Add the cumin seeds followed by the chillies. Fry for 15–20 seconds before adding the peas, the remaining salt and 200ml (7fl oz) of the water. Bring to the boil, reduce the heat to low and cover the pan, then and cook for 5 minutes.

- Leave the peas to cool for a few minutes, then purée them in a food processor or blender with the fresh mint. (If using dried mint, add it later.) Return the purée to the saucepan and add the tomatoes. If you are using dried mint, add it with the tomatoes. Simmer, uncovered, for 2–3 minutes, then remove from the heat and set aside.

- Heat the remaining oil in a non-stick frying pan over medium-high heat. Add the lamb cutlets, shaking off excess marinade as you lift them from the dish. (Reserve the marinade.) Fry the cutlets for 2½ minutes on each side, until browned.

- Mix the remaining water into the leftover marinade and pour this over the cutlets. Stir, then reduce the heat to low and cover the pan. Simmer for 15 minutes. If there is any liquid left at the end of cooking, remove the lid and cook until all the liquid has evaporated.

- Meanwhile, reheat the pea sauce. Transfer the cutlets to a serving dish and pour the sauce over them. Serve at once.

SPICY MEATLOAF WITH CHILLI TOMATO SAUCE

Do not be put off by the time required to prepare and cook this dish. Once the meatloaf is in the oven, you have all the time you need to prepare the accompaniments. Try Spiced Potato Wedges (see page 146), Mashed Potato with Mustard-Speckled Coconut Milk (see page 148) or boiled basmati rice with the meatloaf and offer a raita or salad as well.

SERVES 4

For the meatloaf
675g (1½lb) minced lamb
2–3 large garlic cloves, roughly chopped
2.5cm (1in) cube fresh root ginger, peeled and roughly chopped
1 small onion, roughly chopped
2 tablespoons roughly chopped fresh mint leaves
2–3 tablespoons roughly chopped fresh coriander leaves and stalks
55g (2oz) fresh breadcrumbs
2 tablespoons double cream
1 large egg
1 tablespoon Ground Roasted Coriander (see page 13)
1 teaspoon Gound Roasted Cumin (see page 13)
½ teaspoon grated nutmeg
½–1 teaspoon chilli powder
1 teaspoon salt or to taste

For the chilli tomato sauce
2 tablespoons sunflower oil or vegetable oil
4 garlic cloves, crushed
½ teaspoon ground turmeric
½–1 teaspoon chilli powder
1 teaspoon Ground Roasted Coriander (see page 13)
1 teaspoon Ground Roasted Cumin (see page 13)
1 tablespoon tomato purée
240ml (8fl oz) warm water
½ teaspoon salt or to taste
½ teaspoon sugar
2 small tomatoes, skinned and chopped
2 tablespoons chopped fresh coriander leaves

- Preheat the oven to 190°C/375°F/Gas 5 and grease a 900g (2lb) loaf tin.

- Process all the ingredients for the meatloaf in a food processor until thoroughly combined and smooth. Pack the mixture into the prepared tin and smooth the top. Bake, uncovered, for 50–55 minutes, until the mixture is firm and browned on top.

- To make the chilli tomato sauce, heat the oil in a saucepan over low heat and fry the garlic for 1 minute until lightly browned. Add the turmeric, chilli powder, ground coriander and cumin, and cook for 1 minute.

- Stir in the tomato purée, water, salt and sugar. Bring to the boil, then simmer, uncovered, for 2–3 minutes. Add the tomatoes and cook for a further 2–3 minutes. Stir in the coriander leaves and remove from the heat.

- Drain off the fat from the loaf tin before turning out the meatloaf on to a flat platter or serving plate. Cut the meatloaf into slices and serve the sauce separately.

COOK'S TIP
If the sauce is to be set aside and reheated before you serve the meal, do not stir in the coriander leaves until the sauce has been reheated and is about to be served.

KOFTAS IN HOT LENTIL SAUCE

These delectable koftas (meatballs) are aromatic with mint and coriander, drenched in a smooth lentil sauce, then finished with bright fresh tomatoes and zesty lime juice. Add the exquisite flavour and aroma of plain boiled basmati rice for a meal made in heaven.

SERVES 4

115g (4oz) red lentils (masoor dhal)
4 tablespoons sunflower oil
2.5cm (1in) piece cinnamon stick
4 cloves
2.5cm (1in) cube fresh root ginger, peeled and grated
2–4 green chillies, seeded if liked, chopped
1 tablespoon Meat and Pulses Spice Blend (see page 15)
1½ teaspoons salt or to taste
620ml (21fl oz) hot water
1 large onion, halved and finely sliced

1 large slice white bread, crusts removed
a little milk
30g (1oz) fresh coriander leaves and stalks
450g (1lb) lean minced lamb
1 large egg
2 large garlic cloves
15–20 fresh mint leaves
1 teaspoon garam masala
2 tomatoes, chopped
juice of ½ lime

- Wash the lentils in several changes of water until the water runs clear, then leave to drain in a colander.

- Heat 2 tablespoons of the oil in a heavy-based frying pan (preferably non-stick) over gentle heat. Add the cinnamon, cloves and ginger and half the green chillies. Fry gently for 1 minute, then add the lentils. Stir-fry the lentils for about 1 minute and add the meat and pulses spice blend. Fry for a further 1–2 minutes, then add half the salt and 470ml (15fl oz) of the hot water. Cover the pan and simmer for 15 minutes.

- Meanwhile, heat the remaining oil in a frying pan over medium heat and fry the onion for 10–12 minutes, stirring regularly, until it is well browned. Drain on kitchen paper.

- Put the bread on a plate and trickle enough milk over it to make it quite soggy, then squeeze out and discard all the milk. Put the bread in a food processor.

- Reserve about a quarter of the coriander and roughly chop the remainder, then add it to the bread with the remaining green chillies and salt. Add the lamb, egg, garlic, mint and garam masala to the food processor. Process the ingredients until they form a smooth mixture, then transfer to a bowl. Wash the food-processor bowl.

- When the lentils have cooked for 15 minutes, remove the cinnamon stick and purée them until smooth in the clean food processor or in a blender. Return to the pan and add the remaining hot water, then place over very low heat.

- Have a bowl of cold water into which to dip your hands, then shape the meat mixture into walnut-sized balls. Keep your hands moist to prevent the mixture from sticking to them. As they are shaped, add the koftas to the gently simmering lentils in a single layer.

- When all the koftas are added to the lentils, cover the pan and cook over gentle heat for 20 minutes. Do not stir the koftas for the first 10–12 minutes, but shake the pan gently to ensure they do not stick to the bottom. Once the meat mixture has set and become firm, the koftas can be stirred occasionally for even cooking.

- Meanwhile, chop the reserved coriander leaves and add them to the koftas with the tomatoes and lime juice, then remove from the heat. Serve garnished with the reserved fried onions.

MINCED LAMB WITH GARLIC, CHILLI AND EGGS

In Indian cooking, eggs often take centre stage for lunch or dinner. This recipe of Muslim origin bears a certain resemblance to Spanish tortilla, but, naturally, Indian spices play a major role. Serve chapatis, soft wheat-flour tortillas or Spiced Potato Wedges (see page 146) as an accompaniment.

SERVES 4

450g (1lb) lean minced lamb
4 tablespoons sunflower oil
1 large onion, finely chopped
2.5cm (1in) cube fresh root ginger, peeled and finely grated, or 2 teaspoons Ginger Purée (see page 16)
4–5 garlic cloves, crushed, or 2 teaspoons Garlic Purée (see page 16)
½ teaspoon ground turmeric
1 teaspoon Ground Roasted Coriander (see page 13)

1½ teaspoons Ground Roasted Cumin (see page 13)
1¼ teaspoon salt or to taste
1 teaspoon garam masala
2 tomatoes, chopped
1 small cauliflower, cut into 1cm (½in) florets
90ml (3fl oz) warm water
1–3 green chillies, seeded if liked, finely chopped
3 tablespoons chopped fresh coriander leaves
4 eggs, beaten

- Cook the minced lamb in a non-stick saucepan over medium heat, stirring continuously until it begins to sizzle and give up its fat. Reduce the heat slightly and cook, uncovered, for 9–10 minutes, until dry. Reduce the heat to low and cook, stirring regularly, for 3–4 minutes, until the mince is brown. Remove from the heat and drain off any excess fat.

- Meanwhile, heat the oil in a large frying pan and add the onion. Fry for 8–9 minutes, until beginning to brown, then add the ginger and garlic. Fry for 2–3 minutes, then add the turmeric, ground coriander and cumin. Cook for a further 1–2 minutes.

- Add the browned mince, salt, garam masala and tomatoes to the onion mixture. Continue to cook for 2–3 minutes, then sprinkle in 2 tablespoons water (not the measured water listed above) and cook for a further 2 minutes.

- Add the cauliflower and stir over medium heat for 3–4 minutes. Pour in the warm water and cover the pan, then cook over low heat for 7–8 minutes, until the cauliflower is tender.

- Meanwhile, preheat the grill to high. Stir in the chillies and coriander leaves and make sure the mince mixture is evenly spread out in the pan. Pour the eggs evenly over the meat and cook over low to medium heat until the eggs are just set.

- Place the pan under the grill, about 7.5cm (3in) below the heat source, for 3–4 minutes, until the top of the mixture is browned. Serve at once.

COOK'S TIP
Check that the handle of the frying pan will not burn when the pan is placed under the grill. If necessary, protect your hands with a thick oven glove or cloth and hold the pan under the grill to prevent the handle from being pushed too far under the heat.

DRY-FRIED MINCED LAMB WITH SPINACH AND TOMATO

This recipe is very similar to the *sag gosht* (spinach cooked with lamb) served in most Indian restaurants. The usual cubed lamb takes longer to cook, so I have used mince to make a quick and tasty dish that is ideal for mid-week meals. The recipe is equally successful with minced chicken, turkey or pork.

SERVES 4

4 tablespoons sunflower oil
1 teaspoon cumin seeds
8–10 fenugreek seeds
4 small (bird's eye) red chillies or 1–2 large red chillies, seeded if liked, snipped into small pieces
450g (1lb) lean minced lamb
1 large onion, finely chopped
5cm (2in) cube fresh root ginger, peeled and finely grated, or 1 tablespoon Ginger Purée (see page 16)

4–5 large garlic cloves, crushed, or 1 tablespoon Garlic Purée (see page 16)
1½ tablespoons Meat and Pulses Spice Blend (see page 15)
200g (7oz) can chopped tomatoes
1¼ teaspoon salt or to taste
½ teaspoon sugar
340g (12oz) spinach, chopped, or frozen chopped spinach
150ml (5fl oz) warm water
3 tablespoons single cream

- Heat 1 tablespoon of the oil in a non-stick frying pan over medium heat. Add the cumin seeds and cook for 15–20 seconds before adding the fenugreek seeds and the chillies. Cook until the chillies blacken (darkening in colour rather than burning).

- Add the lamb and continue to cook over medium heat, stirring regularly, until the mince is dry. Reduce the heat slightly and continue to cook until the mince is browned. Remove from the heat and set aside.

- Meanwhile, heat the remaining oil in a large heavy-based saucepan over low heat and fry the onions for 10–12 minutes, stirring regularly, until they are pale golden in colour. Add the ginger and garlic and fry for 1 minute.

- Add the meat and pulses spice blend to the onion mixture and cook for 30–40 seconds, then stir in the tomatoes with their juice. Cook for 4–5 minutes, or until the oil begins to float.

- Stir in the salt, sugar and spinach and the browned mince. Stir over medium-high heat for 2–3 minutes. Pour in the water. Reduce the heat to low, cover and cook for 15 minutes.

- Finally, stir in the cream and remove the pan from the heat. Serve at once, with chapatis or naan.

COOK'S TIP
Kitchen scissors are useful for cutting up chillies as well as herbs, particularly the very small bird's eye chillies. Remember to remove the seeds from chillies if you do not want a very hot dish as they are particularly hot.

LIVER DO-PIAZA

Anyone who enjoys liver will find spiced lamb's liver, cooked with lashings of onion, to be a wonderful treat. Serve chapatis or naan with the liver.

SERVES 4

4–5 tablespoons sunflower oil or vegetable oil

2 large onions, halved and finely sliced

675g (1½lb) lamb's liver

5cm (2in) cube fresh root ginger, peeled and finely grated, or 1 tablespoon Ginger Purée (see page 16)

4–5 large garlic cloves, crushed, or 2½ teaspoons Garlic Purée (see page 16)

350ml (11fl oz) warm water

1½ teaspoons Ground Roasted Coriander (see page 13)

1½ teaspoons Ground Roasted Cumin (see page 13)

1 teaspoon ground turmeric

½–1 teaspoon chilli powder

1 teaspoon salt or to taste

2 tablespoons plain yogurt, whisked

2 tomatoes, chopped

2 fresh red chillies, seeded if liked, cut into julienne strips

2–3 tablespoons chopped fresh coriander leaves

- Heat the oil in a frying pan and fry the onions for 12–14 minutes, until browned. Stir regularly to brown the onions evenly.

- Meanwhile, bring plenty of water to the boil in a saucepan and add the liver. Bring back to the boil and cook for 2–3 minutes, then drain the liver and rinse it thoroughly in cold water. Drain the liver well, then cut it into 1 x 5cm (½ x 2in) strips.

- Use a draining spoon to remove half the browned onions from the pan and set them aside on kitchen paper to drain. Add the ginger and garlic to the onions remaining in the pan and cook for 2 minutes. Pour in 90ml (3fl oz) of the warm water and continue to cook for 1–2 minutes.

- Stir in the coriander, cumin, turmeric and chilli powder. Cook for 1 minute before adding the liver and salt. Stir over medium-high heat for 3–4 minutes, then add half the yogurt. Reduce the heat slightly, cook for 2 minutes and add the remaining yogurt.

- Pour in the remaining water, cover and simmer for 15 minutes. Add the tomatoes and cook, uncovered, over medium heat for 5 minutes. Finally, stir in the chillies and coriander leaves, cook for 1 minute and remove from the heat. Serve at once, garnished with the reserved fried onions.

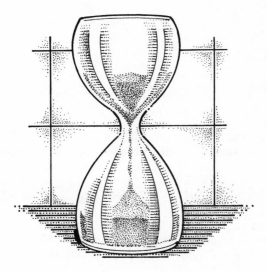

Lamb & Pork

LAMB'S LIVER WITH SPICED BUTTER

Although liver rarely features on restaurant menus, it is cooked frequently in Indian homes. Cooking the liver in butter sauce gives a rich dish that tastes good with boiled basmati rice and a raita.

SERVES 4–5

675g (1½lb) lamb's liver
55g (2oz) unsalted butter
8–10 fenugreek seeds
½ teaspoon onion seeds
4 large garlic cloves, crushed, or 2 teaspoons Garlic Purée (see page 16)
½ teaspoon salt or to taste

85g (3oz) plain yogurt, whisked
1–2 green chillies, seeded if liked, sliced diagonally
300ml (½ pint) Butter Sauce (see page 18)
2 tablespoons chopped fresh coriander leaves

- Rinse the liver and pat it dry on kitchen paper, then cut it into 2.5cm x 5mm (1 x ¼in) strips.

- Melt the butter in a heavy-based frying pan over gentle heat. Add the fenugreek seeds, onion seeds and garlic, then cook gently for 1 minute. Add the liver and stir over medium heat for 4–5 minutes. Then increase the heat to medium-high and cook for 7–8 minutes, stirring regularly, until all the moisture has evaporated and the liver begins to brown.

- Add the salt, yogurt, chillies and butter sauce. Heat until just simmering, cover and cook gently for 15–20 minutes.

- Stir in the coriander leaves and remove from the heat. Serve at once.

BACON OMELETTE

A bacon omelette may not sound like an authentic Indian dish, but this is one example of a range of recipes created by Indian chefs for the British families during the Raj. Have warm plates ready for the omelettes and any accompaniments, such as Garlic Potatoes with Chilli and Mustard (see page 147), and serve with a salad.

SERVES 2

2–3 tablespoons unsalted butter
1 small onion, finely chopped
2–3 rashers unsmoked bacon, rinded and finely chopped
1 green chilli, seeded if liked, finely chopped, or 1 tablespoon finely chopped green pepper

4 eggs, separated
1 small tomato, chopped
2 tablespoons finely chopped fresh coriander leaves or parsley
salt to taste (optional)
freshly ground black pepper

- The above quantities make two individual omelettes, one at a time in a 15–18cm (6–7in) omelette pan. Melt half the butter in the pan and fry half the onion for 3–4 minutes. Add half the bacon and chilli or pepper, and fry for 2–3 minutes.

- Meanwhile, whisk the whites of 2 eggs until frothy, then add the 2 yolks and 2 tablespoons water. Season the eggs with salt (if required) and pepper and beat well. Set aside.

- Add half the tomato and coriander or parsley to the bacon mixture. Increase the heat to high and then pour in the beaten egg to cover the bacon mixture completely. Allow the egg to set for a few seconds, then use a fork or spatula to draw the mixture from the side towards the centre, tilting the pan at the same time to let the uncooked egg mixture run on to the hot pan. Do this until all the uncooked egg has spread to the side of the pan and the set mixture is drawn to the centre.

- Fold the omelette in half or into three. If necessary, roll it over to brown both sides, but this is not usually necessary when the pan is hot enough. Serve immediately. Wipe out the pan with kitchen paper and cook the remaining ingredients to make the second omelette.

HOT SAUSAGE PILAU

An Indo-Portuguese recipe from Goa, this pilau is equally at home on the family table and on the formal dinner-party menu. Hot and spicy Goan pork sausages are used in the authentic version, but I find that any good-quality spicy sausages from the supermarket work well. I occasionally use pork and leek sausages and add fresh red and green chillies with crushed black peppercorns. Raita and pappadums are excellent accompaniments.

SERVES 4

280g (10oz) basmati rice
8 spicy pork or beef sausages
4 tablespoons sunflower oil
2.5cm (1in) piece cinnamon stick
6 green cardamom pods, bruised
6 cloves
1 large onion, halved and finely sliced
3–4 large garlic cloves, crushed, or 2 teaspoons Garlic Purée (see page 16)

1 green chilli, seeded if liked, finely chopped
$1/2$–1 teaspoon chilli powder
$1/2$ teaspoon ground turmeric
$1/2$ teaspoon salt or to taste
500ml (17fl oz) warm water
2 hard-boiled eggs, quartered lengthways

- Wash the rice in several changes of cold water until the water runs clear, then leave it to soak in fresh water to cover for 15 minutes.

- Grill or fry the sausages until well browned and cooked through. Set aside to cool, then cut at a slant into thick slices.

- Heat the oil in a heavy-based saucepan over low heat. Add the cinnamon, cardamoms and cloves. Let the spices sizzle until the cardamom pods are puffed up. Then add the onion and cook for 7–8 minutes until it begins to brown. Stir in the garlic and green chilli and fry for 2–3 minutes. Add the chilli powder and turmeric.

- Drain the rice and add it to the prepared onions and spices. Stir over medium heat for 1–2 minutes, then add the salt and pour in the water. Bring it to the boil over high heat, reduce the heat to medium and cook, uncovered, until the surface water has been absorbed.

- Reduce the heat to very low and cover the pan. Cook for 6–7 minutes, then switch off the heat and leave the pan undisturbed for 5–7 minutes.

- Using a large metal spoon, transfer half the rice to a serving dish. Arrange half the sausages on top and pile the remaining rice on them. Arrange the rest of the sausages on the rice and the egg quarters around the edge.

PORK SAUSAGES IN HOT TOMATO SAUCE

The spicy sausages made in Goa were the inspiration for this recipe, in which lean pork sausages are simmered in a hot and spicy tomato sauce. Serve boiled basmati rice as the main accompaniment, with a side dish, such as Broccoli and Red Pepper Raita (see page 174).

SERVES 4

8 lean pork sausages
2 tablespoons sunflower oil
$\frac{1}{2}$ teaspoon black mustard seeds
$\frac{1}{2}$ teaspoon cumin seeds
1–2 green chillies, seeded if liked, finely chopped
300ml ($\frac{1}{2}$ pint) Northern Curry Sauce or Kadhai Sauce (see page 19)

$\frac{1}{2}$ teaspoon salt or to taste
$\frac{1}{2}$–1 teaspoon chilli powder
225g (8oz) frozen peas
2–3 tablespoons chopped fresh coriander leaves
1 tablespoon lemon juice

- Grill the sausages or shallow fry them over high heat until browned all over. The sausages should not be fully cooked at this stage. Drain on kitchen paper and set aside to cool.

- Meanwhile, heat the oil in a saucepan over medium heat and add the mustard seeds. As soon as they pop, reduce the heat to low and add the cumin seeds and chillies. Fry for 1 minute. Pour in the curry sauce and add the salt and chilli powder. Cook over low to medium heat for 2–3 minutes.

- Slice the sausages thickly at an angle and add to the simmering sauce. Add the peas, stir and cover the pan. Cook over low heat for 8–10 minutes.

- Stir in the coriander leaves and lemon juice, remove from the heat and serve.

Vegetarian Dishes

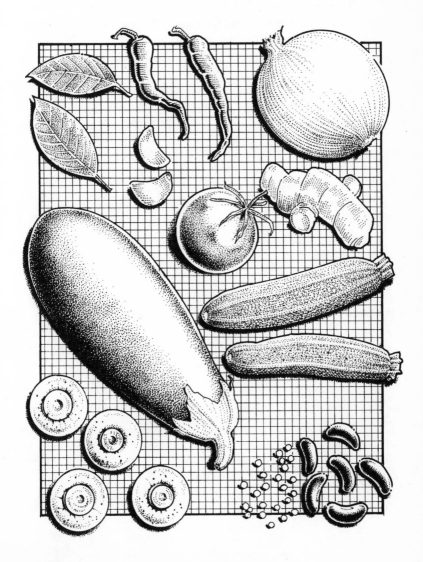

From familiar Tarka Channa Dhal (see page 125) to the more unusual Golden Semolina Pilau (see page 118) or Spiced Aubergine Purée with Eggs (see page 132), this chapter will equip you with all the information needed to present delicious, well-balanced vegetarian meals. The recipes have been carefully chosen for their nutritional qualities, ensuring that they provide protein, carbohydrate, vitamins and the other essential nutrients for a healthy diet.

These dishes are also intended as a source of inspiration. I hope you will be adventurous and change the combination of vegetables, beans and peas to create your own recipes based on the ideas. Many vegetarian recipes are excellent for making quick meals, especially using canned beans and pulses. Canned pulses should be drained and rinsed thoroughly in cold water.

Eggs do not usually feature in Indian vegetarian cooking, but I have used them in this chapter because many Western vegetarian diets include them. Eggs are also particularly useful for quick cooking.

MOONG DHAL PILAU

This quick dish is a meal in itself. Toasted almonds and hard-boiled eggs can be added as a garnish. Serve a raita and some pappadums to make a balanced meal.

SERVES 4

280g (10oz) basmati rice
140g (5oz) moong dhal (skinless split mung beans)
30g (1oz) butter
3 tablespoons sunflower oil or soya oil
2.5cm (1in) piece cinnamon stick
2 bay leaves
1 large onion, halved and thinly sliced

4 large garlic cloves, crushed
1–2 green chillies, seeded if liked, sliced lengthways
1 tablespoon Vegetable and Poultry Spice Blend (see page 14)
$1\frac{1}{2}$ teaspoons salt or to taste
900ml ($1\frac{1}{2}$ pints) hot water

- Wash the rice and dhal together until the water runs clear, then soak in fresh water to cover for 15–20 minutes.

- Meanwhile, heat the butter and oil together in a heavy-based saucepan over low heat and add the cinnamon and bay leaves. Let the spices sizzle gently for 25–30 seconds, then add the onion, garlic and chillies. Increase the heat slightly and fry for 10–12 minutes, until the onion is lightly browned.

- Drain the rice and lentils and add to the onion along with the vegetable and poultry spice blend and salt. Stir-fry for 3–4 minutes, then pour in the water. Stir once and bring to the boil. Boil steadily for 2 minutes, then reduce the heat to very low (use a heat diffuser if necessary), cover the pan and cook for 12 minutes.

- Remove the pan from the heat and set it aside for 6–7 minutes, without removing the lid. Use a large metal spoon to serve the pilau.

GOLDEN SEMOLINA PILAU

This recipe can be cooked at lightning speed. If the idea of semolina in a savoury dish does not immediately appeal, remember that it is the basis for couscous and for a particular type of Italian baked gnocchi. Here, the semolina is dry roasted until golden brown, then cooked with spices to make a delicious low-fat vegetarian meal that is high in carbohydrate. The peas provide a source of fibre and vitamins. The quantities given will serve two hungry people.

SERVES 2

3 tablespoons sunflower oil or vegetable oil
2.5cm (1in) piece cinnamon stick
4 cloves
2 bay leaves, crumbled
1 onion, halved and finely sliced
1–2 green chillies, seeded if liked, finely chopped

115g (4oz) semolina
½ teaspoon ground turmeric
½ teaspoon salt
500ml (17fl oz) warm water
115g (4oz) frozen peas or cooked fresh peas
1 tablespoon lemon juice

- Heat the oil over low heat in a frying pan, preferably with a non-stick surface. Add the cinnamon, cloves and bay leaves, and fry them gently for 25–30 seconds. Then add the onion and chillies, and fry over low to medium heat for 8–9 minutes, stirring regularly, until the onion is well browned.

- Meanwhile, roast the semolina as the onions are cooking. Heat a heavy-based pan over medium heat and add the semolina, then dry roast it for 6–7 minutes, until golden brown. If you do not have a heavy pan, keep the heat down to a low setting to prevent the semolina from scorching. Stir frequently at first, then continuously as the semolina starts to brown to ensure that it cooks evenly. Remove from the heat.

- Add the turmeric and salt to the onions, then stir in the water and peas. Bring to the boil and simmer for 3–4 minutes. Reduce the heat to low and stir in the lemon juice, then add the roasted semolina. Cook, stirring constantly, until the semolina has absorbed all the water and is not sticky. Remove from the heat and serve.

COOK'S TIP
To provide a contrast in texture, serve sprinkled with toasted nuts or Bombay mix. If I want an ingredient that is bland, but crunchy, I sprinkle Rice Krispies over the top – try it, it is surprisingly good (but be sure to use the unsweetened cereal).

CARROT, SPINACH AND CHICK-PEA PILAU

I use frozen leaf spinach which can be chopped quite easily when part-thawed, but if you do not mind spending the time cleaning fresh spinach, use it instead.

SERVES 4

280g (10oz) basmati rice
600ml (1 pint) hot water
1½ teaspoons salt or to taste
2 tablespoons sunflower oil or
  vegetable oil
1 tablespoon unsalted butter
5cm (2in) piece cinnamon stick
6 green cardamom pods, bruised
6 cloves

2 bay leaves
1 large onion, finely sliced
1 tablespoon Vegetable and Poultry
  Spice Blend (see page 14)
225g (8oz) spinach leaves, fresh or
  frozen, chopped
400g (14oz) can chick peas,
  drained and rinsed
1 large carrot, coarsely grated

- Wash the rice in several changes of water and then soak it for 15 minutes. Drain thoroughly and put into a saucepan. Add the water and 1 teaspoon of the salt. Bring to the boil, then reduce the heat to medium-low. Cover and cook for 3–4 minutes, until the surface water has evaporated. Reduce the heat to very low and cook for a further 4 minutes. Remove from the heat and set aside.

- Meanwhile, heat the oil and butter together in a large frying pan over low heat. Add the cinnamon, cardamoms, cloves and bay leaves. When the cardamom pods have puffed up, add the onion and increase the heat to medium-high. Fry, stirring regularly, for 9–10 minutes, until the onions are lightly browned.

- Add the vegetable and poultry spice blend and cook for 1 minute. Add the spinach and chick peas, and stir until the spinach has softened or wilted, then add the carrots and the remaining salt. Stir once.

- Pile the cooked rice on top of the vegetables and cook, uncovered, for 2–3 minutes. Remove from the heat and mix gently using a metal spoon, then serve.

PLAIN BOILED BASMATI RICE

Use the quantities of rice and water above and follow the first step of the method. Increase the cooking time slightly to 5 minutes (instead of 4 minutes) once the heat is reduced to very low. Then leave the rice to rest for 6–7 minutes without removing the lid before serving.

BABY CORN AND CHICK-PEA KORMA

You are sure to impress vegetarian friends by serving this stunning dish, which is visually appealing and appetizing as well as being easy to cook. Serve Saffron Rice (see page 194) and Chunky Tomatoes in Mellow Coconut Sauce (see page 154) or Coconut-Coated Cucumber with Mustard and Lime (see page 145) as accompaniments.

SERVES 4

55g (2oz) unsalted cashew nut pieces

150ml (5fl oz) boiling water

4 tablespoons sunflower oil

225g (8oz) shallots, finely chopped

2.5cm (1in) cube fresh root ginger, peeled and grated, or 2 teaspoons Ginger Purée (see page 16)

3–4 large garlic cloves, crushed, or 2 teaspoons Garlic Purée (see page 16)

1 tablespoon Ground Roasted Coriander (see page 13)

1 teaspoon Ground Roasted Cumin (see page 13)

1/4 teaspoon ground turmeric

1/2–1 teaspoon chilli powder

225g (8oz) baby corn, cut into 2–3 pieces

400g (14oz) can chick peas, drained and rinsed

240ml (8fl oz) warm water

150ml (5fl oz) single cream

1 1/2 tablespoons lemon juice

- Place the cashew nuts in a bowl. Add the boiling water and set aside.

- Heat the oil in a saucepan and fry the shallots for 5–6 minutes. Then add the ginger and garlic, and fry for a further 2–3 minutes, stirring continuously.

- Stir in the coriander, cumin, turmeric and chilli powder, reduce the heat to low and cook for 2 minutes. Add the corn and chick peas and pour in the water. Bring to the boil, cover the pan and cook for 10–12 minutes.

- Meanwhile, purée the cashews in their soaking water in a food processor or blender, then add to the corn and chick peas. Stir in the cream and bring back to a gentle simmer. Cook gently, uncovered, for 4–5 minutes. Stir in the lemon juice and serve.

MASALA CHANNA DHAL WITH COURGETTES

You can buy channa dhal from health food shops as well as Indian stores. Though yellow split peas are similar in appearance, their taste is not the same. Because I like channa dhal *al dente*, with a bit of bite, rather than cooked until very soft, I do not soak them before cooking. Serve naan or Ginger, Turmeric and Coriander Rice (see page 192) with the dhal.

SERVES 4

225g (8oz) channa dhal or yellow split peas
600ml (1 pint) hot water
2 tablespoons unsalted butter
4–5 shallots, chopped
1 teaspoon Ground Roasted Coriander (see page 13)
225g (8oz) courgettes, cut into small cubes

½ teaspoon salt or to taste
300ml (½ pint) Butter Sauce (see page 18)
1–2 firm tomatoes, chopped
2 tablespoons double cream
2–3 tablespoons chopped fresh coriander leaves

- Wash the dhal or yellow split peas well and drain. Put into a saucepan and add the hot water. Cook over low to medium heat, uncovered, for 20 minutes, by which time most of the water should have evaporated, leaving about 1 tablespoon.

- Melt the butter gently over low heat and fry the shallots for 4–5 minutes, until softened. Add the ground coriander and cook for 30 seconds.

- Add the dhal and stir over medium heat for 2–3 minutes, then add the courgettes, salt and butter sauce. Cover the pan and cook over low heat for 5–6 minutes.

- Add the tomatoes, cream and coriander. Cook, uncovered, for 1–2 minutes and remove from the heat.

BENGAL TARKA DHAL

This is a popular Bengali method of transforming humble red
lentils into a superbly flavoured dish with just a few simple
ingredients. This dhal is especially good with boiled basmati rice
and a dry-spiced fish, meat or vegetable dish.

SERVES 4

225g (8oz) red lentils (masoor
dhal)
1 teaspoon ground turmeric
1 litre (1³/₄ pints) hot water
1¹/₄ teaspoons salt or to taste
1 tablespoon sunflower oil or
vegetable oil

1 teaspoon Five-Spice Mix (see
page 13)
1–2 green chillies, seeded if liked,
chopped
2–3 tablespoons chopped fresh
coriander leaves
1 small tomato, chopped

- Wash the lentils well, then drain them and place in a saucepan with
the turmeric. Add and water and bring to the boil. Reduce the heat
to just below medium and cook, uncovered, for 7–8 minutes. Cover
the pan and reduce the heat to low. Simmer for 18–20 minutes. Stir
in the salt.

- Heat the oil in a small saucepan. When hot, but not smoking, add
the five-spice mix followed by the chillies. Cook for 15–20 seconds
and then stir in the coriander leaves and tomatoes. Cook for
1 minute.

- Add the spice and tomato mixture to the cooked lentils. Stir and
serve at once.

TARKA CHANNA DHAL

This very simple, but superbly flavoured, lentil dish can be cooked quite effortlessly. Naan or chapatis and a vegetable dish go well with the dhal. A chutney or raita can be served instead of the vegetable dish. When served with rice, this dhal is also an excellent accompaniment to any fairly dry fish, poultry or meat dish.

SERVES 4

225g (8oz) channa dhal or yellow split peas
1 teaspoon ground turmeric
900ml (1½ pints) hot water
¾ teaspoon salt or to taste
1 tablespoon sunflower oil or vegetable oil
2.5cm (1in) piece cinnamon stick
4 green cardamom pods, bruised
4 cloves
2 bay leaves, crumpled
1–2 small dried red chillies (bird's eye chillies)
1 green chilli, seeded if liked, chopped
1–2 small tomatoes, chopped
2–3 tablespoons chopped fresh coriander leaves

• Wash and drain the dhal well, then place them in a saucepan with the turmeric. Pour in the water and bring to the boil. Reduce the heat to medium and cook, uncovered, for 9–10 minutes. Cover the pan and cook over low heat for 20–25 minutes.

• Stir in the salt, switch off the heat and mash some of the dhal with a potato masher to thicken the mixture. The dhal should be the consistency of mango chutney: if it is too thick, add a little water.

• Heat the oil in a small saucepan over low heat. Fry the cinnamon, cardamoms, cloves, bay leaves and both types of chilli for 25–30 seconds. Add the tomatoes and cook over medium heat for about 1 minute.

• Add the the spice mixture to the dhal with the coriander leaves. Stir over low heat for 1–2 minutes before serving.

COOK'S TIP
The dhal is a healthy vegetarian main dish, being high in protein and fibre, but low in calories, with a negligible amount of fat. You can use yellow split peas, but buy channa dhal if you can because they have a distinctive, nutty flavour.

BEANS AND MUSHROOMS IN CHILLI TOMATO SAUCE

This dish provides a good combination of flavour, texture and nutritional value as well as visual appeal. I use button mushrooms, but you may like to be a little more adventurous and try other varieties, such as shiitake, morel or other wild mushrooms.

SERVES 4

3 tablespoons sunflower oil
1 large onion, finely chopped
2 small tomatoes, chopped
300ml (½ pint) Northern Curry Sauce or Kadhai Sauce (see page 19)
½ teaspoon salt or to taste

340g (12oz) button mushrooms
400g (14oz) can kidney beans, drained and rinsed
1–2 green chillies, seeded and cut into julienne strips
2–3 tablespoons chopped fresh coriander leaves

- Heat the oil in a saucepan and fry the onion for 10–12 minutes, stirring regularly, until soft and lightly browned.

- Add the tomatoes and cook for 3–4 minutes. Pour in half the curry sauce and cook, uncovered, over medium-high heat for 2–3 minutes. Repeat with the remaining sauce.

- Stir in the salt, mushrooms and beans. Cover and cook over low heat for 15–20 minutes.

- Finally, add the chillies and coriander leaves. Remove from the heat and serve.

GRILLED PANEER MASALA WITH GARDEN PEAS

This is a variation on traditional mutter paneer. Paneer or halloumi cheese tastes splendid when grilled and simmered in butter sauce. The result is a delicious and elegant vegetarian main course. Saffron Rice (see page 194) or naan is a suitable accompaniment.

SERVES 4

250g (9oz) paneer or halloumi cheese, cut into 2.5cm (1in) wide strips

3 tablespoons sunflower oil or vegetable oil

4–5 shallots, chopped

1cm ($^1/_2$in) cube fresh root ginger, peeled and grated, or 1 teaspoon Ginger Purée (see page 16)

300ml ($^1/_2$ pint) Butter Sauce (see page 18)

225g (8oz) frozen peas

$^1/_2$ teaspoon garam masala

salt to taste

- Preheat the grill to high and line a grill pan with foil. Brush with a little oil.

- Place the cheese on the grill pan. Pour 2 tablespoons of the oil into a frying pan and set aside, then brush half the remaining oil over the cheese. Grill the cheese until browned, then turn the strips, brush with the remaining oil and grill the second side until browned.

- Meanwhile, heat the reserved oil in the pan over medium heat and fry the shallots and ginger for 4–5 minutes. Add the butter sauce and the peas. Bring to a slow simmer, cover and cook gently for 4–5 minutes.

- Cut the strips of cheese across into 2.5cm (1in) squares. Add the cheese to the pan, cover and cook for 2–3 minutes. Stir in the garam masala, taste and add salt if necessary, then serve.

SPICY POTATO FINGERS WITH WHOLE EGGS

You would not be completely wrong to think of this as the Indian equivalent of egg and chips, but the potato fingers are not deep-fried and the eggs are cooked with the potatoes. It makes an easy and satisfying main meal. Serve a salad as an accompaniment or offer Khurmi Naan (see page 167) or garlic bread with the eggs and potatoes.

SERVES 4

4 tablespoons sunflower oil
1 large onion, halved and finely sliced
1–3 green chillies, seeded if liked, chopped or sliced
1 teaspoon ground turmeric
$\frac{1}{2}$–1 teaspoon chilli powder (optional)
1 teaspoon Ground Roasted Coriander (see page 13)

675g (1$\frac{1}{2}$lb) potatoes, cut into 5mm x 5cm ($\frac{1}{4}$ x 2in) fingers
1 teaspoon salt or to taste
15g ($\frac{1}{2}$oz) fresh coriander leaves and stalks, finely chopped
4 large eggs
salt and freshly ground black pepper to taste

- Heat the oil in a non-stick frying pan and fry the onion and chillies for 5–6 minutes.

- Add the turmeric, chilli powder (if using) and ground coriander. Cook for 30 seconds, then add the potatoes and salt. Stir for 1–2 minutes and sprinkle with 3–4 tablespoons water. Reduce the heat to low, cover and cook for 7–8 minutes. Stir the potatoes and add 3–4 tablespoons water as before. Cook for a further 7–8 minutes, stirring once or twice.

- Stir in the coriander leaves and smooth the surface of the potatoes. Break the eggs on to the potato fingers, evenly apart in the pan. Season with salt and pepper. Cover and cook over low heat for 7–8 minutes until the eggs are set. Remove from the heat and serve.

Real Fast Indian Food

EGGS IN CURRY-LEAF COCONUT MILK

This superb recipe comes from the southern state of Kerala. It is simple, quick and satisfying. Serve with boiled basmati rice and a raita, such as White Radish and Carrot Raita (see page 178) or Broccoli and Red Pepper Raita (see page 174). Fresh curry leaves are the key ingredient, but if you do not have any in your freezer, use the dried ones.

SERVES 6

4–5 tablespoons sunflower oil or vegetable oil
1 large onion, finely chopped
2.5cm (1in) cube fresh root ginger, peeled and grated, or
  2 teaspoons Ginger Purée (see page 16)
3–4 garlic cloves, crushed, or
  2 teaspoons Garlic Purée (see page 16)
1–2 green chillies, seeded if liked, sliced lengthways

450g (1lb) potatoes, quartered
240ml (8fl oz) warm water
1 teaspoon salt or to taste
6 hard-boiled eggs
240ml (8fl oz) canned coconut milk
2–3 whole green chillies
2 tablespoons fresh curry leaves
2 small tomatoes, chopped
2–3 tablespoons chopped fresh coriander leaves

• Heat the oil in a large saucepan over medium heat. Fry the onion, ginger, garlic and chillies for 6–7 minutes, until the onion is soft, but not brown.

• Add the potatoes, water and salt. Bring to the boil, cover and cook for 12–15 minutes.

• Meanwhile, make 3–4 incisions into the whites of the eggs without cutting right through them. Add the eggs to the potatoes with the coconut milk and chillies. Cover and cook over low to medium heat for about 5 minutes or until the potatoes are tender.

• Add the curry leaves, tomatoes and coriander. Simmer, uncovered, for 2–3 minutes and serve.

EGG PILAU

This recipe is fast and delicious and makes a completely balanced meal when served with a raita. Offer pappadums to bring a welcome change of texture between mouthfuls of pilau. Besan (chick-pea flour), adds a delicious nuttiness to the spicy batter coating the eggs, but plain flour can be used instead.

SERVES 4

280g (10oz) basmati rice
1¼ teaspoons salt or to taste
1 tablespoon Vegetable and Poultry Spice Blend (see page 14)
1 tablespoon plain yogurt
2 tablespoons besan (gram or chick-pea flour), sifted
1 large egg, beaten
sunflower oil for shallow frying, plus 2 tablespoons
4 hard-boiled eggs, halved lengthways

1 tablespoon butter
1 large onion, finely sliced
2.5cm (1in) cube fresh root ginger, peeled and finely grated, or 2 teaspoons Ginger Purée (see page 16)
1–2 green chillies, seeded if liked, finely chopped
5cm (2in) piece cinnamon stick
4 cloves
2 bay leaves
600ml (1 pint) hot water

- Wash the rice gently in cold water until the water runs clear, then drain well. Spread out the rice on a large plate and sprinkle with 1 teaspoon of the salt and 2 teaspoons of the vegetable and poultry spice blend. Add the yogurt and mix thoroughly, then set aside for 15–20 minutes.

- Meanwhile, blend the besan with a little water to make a smooth, thick paste. Add the beaten egg, a little at a time, while you whisk with a fork to make a smooth batter. Whisk in the remaining salt and spice blend.

- Pour the oil for shallow frying into a frying pan to a depth of about 2.5cm (1in). Dip each hard-boiled egg half in the spiced batter and add to the hot oil. Fry the eggs until well browned all over, turning as necessary. Drain on kitchen paper.

- Heat the 2 tablespoons oil and the butter in a heavy saucepan (preferably non-stick) over medium heat. Add the remaining ingredients, except the water. Fry for 10–12 minutes, until the onions are brown.

- Add the rice and stir for 2–3 minutes, then pour in the hot water. Bring to the boil and cook for 4–6 minutes, until the surface water evaporates. Arrange the fried eggs on top, reduce the heat to very low (use a heat diffuser if necessary) and cover the pan. Cook for 2–3 minutes. Remove from the heat and allow the pilau to rest for 5–6 minutes before serving.

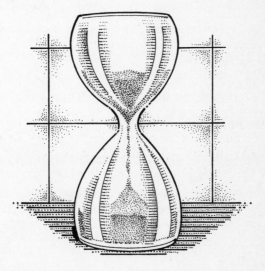

Vegetarian Dishes

Spiced Aubergine Purée with Eggs

Although the aubergine is normally puréed for this dish, I prefer to mash it lightly. Serve chapatis with the purée or offer it as an accompaniment to a rice and lentil dish.

SERVES 4

2 aubergines, about 550g (1¼lb)

3 tablespoons sunflower oil or vegetable oil

1 large onion, finely chopped

2.5cm (1in) cube fresh root ginger, peeled and grated, or 2 teaspoons Ginger Purée (see page 16)

1–2 green chillies, seeded if liked, chopped

½ teaspoon ground turmeric

¼–½ teaspoon chilli powder (optional)

4 hard-boiled eggs

1 teaspoon salt or to taste

2–3 tablespoons chopped fresh coriander leaves

- Score the surface of the aubergines several times, leaving the stems intact. They can be grilled or cooked in a microwave. Grill them for 10–12 minutes, turning once, or allow about 8 minutes in the microwave on high, turning once. If you are using a combination microwave, the aubergines will also brown. Alternatively, cook them on a wire rack over a gas burner for 12–15 minutes, turning them frequently. Leave until cool enough to handle, then peel away the skin and remove the stems. Lightly mash the flesh with a fork.

- Heat the oil in a frying pan and fry the onion, ginger and chillies for 8–10 minutes, until lightly browned. Stir in the turmeric and chilli powder (if using).

- Meanwhile, shell and halve the eggs and remove the yolks. Lightly mash the yolks and chop the whites. Set aside.

- Add the aubergine and salt to the onion mixture and stir over medium heat for 6–8 minutes. Add the egg yolks and cook for 2–3 minutes, then add the egg whites and the coriander leaves. Cook for 1–2 minutes before serving.

GRILLED MUSHROOM OMELETTE

Served with Spiced Potato Wedges (see page 146) and a salad, this makes a delicious and nutritious meal with the minimum of effort.

SERVES 2

4 eggs
2 tablespoons sunflower oil
2 shallots, finely chopped
1 fresh red or green chilli, seeded if liked, finely chopped
115g (4oz) button mushrooms, sliced

2–3 tablespoons finely chopped fresh coriander leaves
salt and freshly ground black pepper

- Preheat the grill to medium. Beat the eggs with 2 tablespoons cold water, season to taste and set aside.

- Heat the oil in a 15–18cm (6–7in) omelette pan over medium heat and fry the shallots and chilli for 3–4 minutes.

- Add the mushrooms and fry for a further 2–3 minutes. Stir in the coriander leaves, then season with salt and pepper.

- Gradually pour in the eggs to cover the mushroom mixture completely. Cook for 2–3 minutes until set underneath. Transfer the pan to the grill, about 12cm (5in) below the heat source, and cook the omelette until set and golden brown. Cut into wedges and serve.

Salads & Vegetables

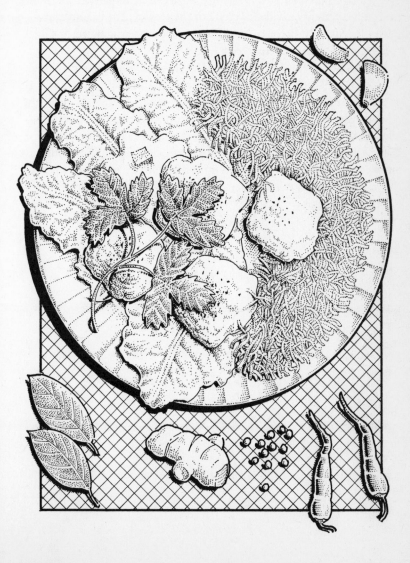

Most people associate Indian food with autumn and winter, when a substantial, hot and spicy meal brings warmth to cold days. Of course, there is also a wide variety of Indian dishes to suit warm seasons, selected not only according to cooking method, but also by the spices used in the recipes. The substantial salads included in this chapter are perfect for relaxed summer eating or occasions when you want a light and refreshing main course.

Bread is the only accompaniment necessary for most of the delicious spiced salads in this chapter. Apart from Indian breads, many European specialities will complement the recipes. For example, try Italian breads with herbs or sun-dried tomatoes, garlic bread or Greek bread topped with crunchy seeds.

When a hot main meal is served, the side dishes and accompaniments often steal the scene. Presenting a selection of dishes providing variety in taste, texture and colour to complement the main dish is one of the interesting features of Indian menus. Accompaniments are carefully selected to enhance the main food: for example, rich dishes should be teamed with simply spiced recipes for clean, or refreshing, flavours. Simple main dishes can be served with others that are more complex. There are recipes in this chapter to complete both vegetarian and meat-based menus.

TANGY POTATO AND CHICK-PEA SALAD

This is one of the most popular street foods in northern India. *Chaat*, as it is known, is eaten as an appetizer or snack, but as it provides plenty of dietary fibre, protein and other essential nutrients, it is also ideal as a main course.

SERVES 4

juice of ½ lemon or
   2–3 tablespoons tamarind juice
15g (½oz) fresh coriander leaves
   and stalks
15g (½oz) fresh mint leaves
2–4 green chillies, seeded if liked,
   chopped
1 small onion, roughly chopped
2 heaped tablespoons ground
   almonds or desiccated coconut,
   ground in a coffee grinder
1 teaspoon salt or to taste
1½ teaspoons soft brown sugar
4 cloves

1 teaspoon black peppercorns
1 teaspoon cumin seeds
2 tablespoons sunflower oil or
   vegetable oil
450g (1lb) potatoes, cut into small
   cubes, cooked and cooled
2 x 400g (14oz) cans chick peas,
   drained and rinsed
To serve
plain mild yogurt or Greek-style
   yogurt
Bombay mix or garlic and herb
   croûtons

- Blend the lemon juice or tamarind, coriander leaves and stalks, mint, chillies and onion in a food processor or blender. Add 2–3 tablespoons water and purée until smooth, then add the almonds or coconut, salt and sugar. Blend for a few seconds and set aside.

- Put the cloves, peppercorns and cumin seeds into a small plastic bag and crush them lightly with a rolling pin.

- Heat the oil in a small saucepan over medium heat and add the crushed spices. Fry for 25–30 seconds and switch off the heat.

- Put the potatoes and the chick peas into a large mixing bowl and add the puréed ingredients and the fried spices. Mix thoroughly and serve topped with yogurt and Bombay mix or croûtons.

MEATBALLS AND NEW POTATOES IN SPICED YOGURT

With a glass of your favourite wine, beer or other drink, some home-made or shop-bought flavoured bread, this salad is the ideal choice for a relaxed *al fresco* meal.

SERVES 4

1cm (½in) cube fresh root ginger, peeled and roughly chopped

2–3 garlic cloves

1 teaspoon garam masala

1 large slice white bread, crusts removed

60ml (2fl oz) milk

2 green chillies

450g (1lb) lean minced chicken, turkey or pork

1 small onion, roughly chopped

3–4 tablespoons roughly chopped fresh coriander leaves

2 tablespoons chopped fresh mint leaves

1½ teaspoons salt or to taste

3 tablespoons sunflower oil

150ml (5fl oz) warm water

450g (1lb) mild plain yogurt

½ teaspoon black mustard seeds

½ teaspoon cumin seeds

½ teaspoon crushed dried chillies

450g (1lb) small new potatoes, boiled and cooled

½ teaspoon Ground Roasted Cumin (see page 13)

¼ teaspoon paprika or chilli powder

To serve

lettuce leaves

grated carrots

- Put the ginger, garlic, garam masala, bread and milk into a food processor. Roughly chop and add 1 chilli. Process until the mixture is smooth. Add the mince, onion, coriander and mint and half the salt. Blend until smooth and transfer the mixture to a bowl.

- To shape the meatballs, have a bowl of cold water by your side and dip your hands in it occasionally to stop the mixture from sticking to them. The mixture makes 18 meatballs – it is easier to divide it in half and shape 9 meatballs from each half. They should be about the size of limes. Make the balls round and smooth by rolling them between your palms.

- Heat 2 tablespoons of the oil in a non-stick frying pan over medium heat. Fry the meatballs in a single layer for 5–6 minutes until browned, turning around frequently. Add the water and bring to the boil over high heat. Cook for 5–6 minutes, stirring and turning the meatballs frequently, until all the water has evaporated and the oil remains. Remove from the heat and allow to cool.

- Meanwhile, pour the yogurt into a large bowl and beat until smooth. Crush the remaining green chilli with the salt and add to the yogurt.

- Heat the remaining oil in a small pan over medium heat. Switch off the heat and add the mustard seeds followed by the cumin seeds and dried chillies. Let the spices sizzle for 15–20 seconds and then stir them into the yogurt.

- Add the potatoes and the cooled meatballs to the yogurt and mix thoroughly. Serve on a bed of crisp lettuce leaves. Add a border of grated carrots. Sprinkle the cumin and the paprika or chilli powder on top and serve.

Salads & Vegetables

PINEAPPLE SALAD WITH CHICKEN BHUNA

During a recent trip to India, I came across this delicious salad at a buffet lunch. My version is designed to make summer cooking enjoyable and exciting. Make the salad at least an hour before you intend serving it so that the pineapple has time to tenderize the chicken and give it that melt-in-the-mouth texture. Serve any home-made or shop-bought flavoured bread as an accompaniment.

SERVES 4

2 tablespoons sunflower oil
4–5 large garlic cloves, crushed, or 2 teaspoons Garlic Purée (see page 16)
1–2 green chillies, seeded if liked, finely chopped
4 boneless chicken breasts, about 675g (1½lb), skinned and cut into 1cm (½ in) cubes
1½ teaspoons Ground Roasted Coriander (see page 13)

1½ teaspoons Ground Roasted Cumin (see page 13)
1–2 teaspoons chilli powder
1½ teaspoons salt or to taste
3 tablespoons white wine vinegar
3–4 tablespoons chopped fresh coriander leaves
1 small ripe pineapple
225g (8oz) mild plain yogurt

- Heat the oil in a frying pan over low heat. Fry the garlic and chillies gently for 1 minute. Add the chicken and stir over medium-high heat for 3–4 minutes, until the chicken is opaque. Reduce the heat slightly.

- Reserve a little of the roasted coriander, cumin and chilli powder and add the remainder to the chicken. Add 1 teaspoon of the salt and cook for 2–3 minutes. Add the vinegar and continue to stir for 3–4 minutes. Stir in the coriander leaves, remove from the heat and allow to cool.

- Meanwhile, trim and peel the pineapple. Halve the flesh lengthways, cut out the hard core, then slice both halves and cut the slices into 1cm (½in) wedges.

- Beat the yogurt in a large bowl until smooth. Add the pineapple and the cooled chicken with all the cooking residue from the pan. Stir well and taste for seasoning, adding more salt if necessary.

- Transfer to a serving dish and sprinkle with the reserved coriander, cumin and chilli powder. Cover and leave to stand in a cool place for at least 1 hour before serving.

POTATO PAKORA SALAD

Do not be put off by the length of the ingredients list for this recipe – the preparation and cooking times could not be faster. The pakoras are served with two relishes, both of which can be made in a few minutes.

SERVES 4

450g (1lb) potatoes, freshly cooked
85g (3oz) besan (gram or chick-pea flour)
40g (1½oz) cornmeal
1 teaspoon salt or to taste
1 teaspoon fennel seeds
2–4 green chillies, seeded if liked, finely chopped
115g (4oz) green cabbage, chopped
1 large onion, chopped
2–3 tablespoons chopped fresh coriander leaves and stalks
200–240ml (7–8fl oz) water
sunflower oil for deep-frying

Tamarind relish
1 teaspoon tamarind concentrate or 2 tablespoons tamarind juice

½–1 teaspoon chilli powder
1 teaspoon Ground Roasted Cumin (see page 13)
1½–2 tablespoons soft dark brown sugar
½ teaspoon salt or to taste

Yogurt relish
175g (6oz) Greek-style yogurt
2 teaspoons sugar
½ teaspoon salt or to taste
1 tablespoon finely chopped fresh coriander leaves
6–8 finely chopped fresh mint leaves
Bombay mix or garlic and herb croûtons to serve

• Crush the potatoes lightly with a fork. Some of the potatoes should be mashed, but more should be left in small pieces.

• Mix the besan, cornmeal, salt and fennel in a large bowl. Add the chillies, cabbage, onion and chopped coriander. Stir in the potatoes and gradually add the water, adding enough to bind the mixture into a thick batter.

• Heat the oil for deep-frying to 190°C/375°F or until a cube of day-old bread browns in 45 seconds. Add dessertspoonfuls of the pakora batter to the hot oil, adding enough to cook a batch of pakoras in a single layer. Fry for about 5 minutes, until well browned. Drain on kitchen paper and continue cooking the remaining mixture in batches.

- For the tamarind relish, dissolve the tamarind concentrate in 2 tablespoons hot water. If using tamarind juice, mix it with 2 tablespoons cold water. Add the remaining ingredients and mix well.

- For the yogurt relish, beat the yogurt with a fork and thoroughly mix in all the remaining ingredients.

- To serve, arrange a portion of pakoras on a plate and top with both relishes. Sprinkle Bombay mix or croûtons on top and serve.

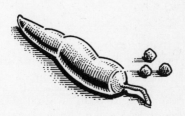

PANEER, AVOCADO AND MANGO SALAD

This superb combination of ingredients can be assembled quickly to make a main course, or it can be offered in small quantities as a side dish.

SERVES 4

2 tablespoons sunflower oil
1 teaspoon cumin seeds
$1/2$–1 teaspoon crushed dried chillies
250g (9oz) paneer or halloumi cheese, cut into bite-sized pieces
$1/2$ teaspoon Ground Roasted Cumin (see page 13)
$1/2$ teaspoon Ground Roasted Coriander (see page 13)
2 tablespoons finely chopped fresh coriander leaves

1 tablespoon finely chopped fresh mint leaves
2 medium avocados
juice of $1/2$ lemon
2 ripe, but firm, mangoes
seeds from 1 pomegranate (optional)
salt to taste
crisp lettuce leaves to serve

• Heat the oil in a frying pan over medium heat and add the cumin seeds, followed by the crushed chillies. Immediately add the cheese and fry over medium-high heat for 3–4 minutes, until browned.

• Switch off the heat and sprinkle in the ground cumin and coriander, then stir in the coriander leaves and mint. If you are using paneer, add salt to taste; halloumi is sometimes quite salty, so you may not want to add any with this cheese. Leave to cool.

• Meanwhile, halve, stone and peel the avocado, then cut it into fairly small cubes and toss with the lemon juice.

• Peel the mangoes and cut the flesh off the central stones, then cut it into pieces similar in size to the avocado. Add the avocado, mango and half the pomegranate seeds (if using) to the cooled cheese. Mix gently and thoroughly so that the spices coat the fruit.

• Arrange a bed of crisp lettuce leaves on a serving plate. Spoon the salad on top and sprinkle the remaining pomegranate seeds (if using) on top.

COCONUT-COATED CUCUMBER WITH MUSTARD AND LIME

In India, cucumber is used in the same way as any other vegetable for hot or cold dishes. This simple salad makes a quick and delicious side dish for almost any main course.

SERVES 4

1 cucumber, peeled if liked, finely chopped
1 teaspoon made English mustard
2 tablespoons desiccated coconut
2 small green chillies, seeded if liked, chopped

1½ tablespoons lime juice
2 teaspoons sunflower oil or vegetable oil
½ teaspoon black mustard seeds
½ teaspoon onion seeds
½ teaspoon salt or to taste

- Put the cucumber in a bowl and add the mustard.

- Grind the coconut and chillies in a coffee mill, or in a mortar using a pestle. Add to the cucumber with the lime juice and mix thoroughly.

- Heat the oil in a small saucepan until hot, but not smoking, then add the mustard seeds. As soon as the seeds crackle, switch off the heat and add the onion seeds. Then pour the mixture over the cucumber and stir thoroughly. Stir in the salt just before serving.

SPICED POTATO WEDGES

These lightly spiced potato wedges make an excellent side dish for all sorts of kababs, fried fish and koftas. They also make a delicious snack when served with Apple and Coconut Chutney (see page 173).

SERVES 4

1kg (2¼lb) new potatoes, scrubbed and cut into wedges
4 tablespoons sunflower oil
salt and freshly ground black pepper to taste
3–4 garlic cloves, crushed
2 bay leaves, cut into pieces
½ teaspoon Ground Roasted Cumin (see page 13)
½ teaspoon Ground Roasted Coriander (see page 13)
½ teaspoon chilli powder

- Preheat the oven to 220°C/425°F/Gas 7.

- Thoroughly dry the potatoes with a clean tea-towel, then place them in a roasting tin. Drizzle the oil all over the potatoes and season them with salt and pepper. Add the garlic and bay leaves, and stir well.

- Bake the potatoes just above the centre of the oven for 20–25 minutes. Sprinkle the cumin, coriander and chilli powder over the potatoes, stir well and return them to the oven for 1 minute. Serve at once.

GARLIC POTATOES WITH CHILLI AND MUSTARD

Use a non-stick pan if you want to cook these potato fingers in the minimum amount of oil.

SERVES 4

675g (1½lb) potatoes
3 tablespoons sunflower oil
½ teaspoon black mustard seeds
½ teaspoon onion seeds
6 large garlic cloves, crushed, or
   2½ teaspoons Garlic Purée (see
   page 16)

1–1½ teaspoons crushed dried
   chillies or chilli powder
1 teaspoon salt or to taste

- Cut the potatoes into fingers, the same thickness as French fries, but half their length. Wash, drain and dry thoroughly with a clean tea-towel.

- Heat the oil in a large frying pan. When hot, but not smoking, add the mustard seeds. As soon as the seeds crackle, reduce the heat to low and add the onion seeds. Fry for 10–15 seconds.

- Add the garlic and chillies, and fry over gentle heat until the garlic is lightly browned. Add the potatoes and salt, and stir over medium heat for 2–3 minutes. Reduce the heat slightly, cover the pan and cook for 8–9 minutes, until the potatoes are tender.

- Remove the lid and increase the heat slightly. Cook, stirring frequently, until the potatoes are browned. Remove from the heat and serve with chapatis or as an accompaniment.

MASHED POTATO WITH MUSTARD-SPECKLED COCONUT MILK

Coconut milk adds an exotic touch to potatoes. Single cream is a good alternative if you do not like coconut.

SERVES 4

1kg (2¼lb) potatoes, freshly cooked
200ml (7fl oz) canned coconut milk
½ teaspoon salt or to taste
1 tablespoon sunflower oil or vegetable oil

½ teaspoon black mustard seeds
½ teaspoon cumin seeds
½ teaspoon dried chilli flakes

- Mash the potatoes lightly, leaving some small whole pieces of potato. Gently heat the coconut milk and salt in a saucepan until it begins to bubble. Add the potatoes and mix thoroughly.

- Heat the oil over medium heat in a small saucepan. Switch off the heat and add the mustard seeds, followed by the cumin seeds, then the chilli flakes (in that order). Let the spices pop and crackle for 15–20 seconds, then pour them over the potatoes. Stir to mix thoroughly and serve.

COOK'S TIP
The potatoes can be cooked in the microwave. Slice them thickly and cook them with 2 tablespoons water for about 15 minutes on high. Stir to rearrange the potatoes at least once, then leave to stand for 5–6 minutes. While the potatoes are cooking you will be free to get on with another part of the recipe.

SPINACH AND SWEET POTATOES IN A CREAMY BUTTER SAUCE

The distinct flavour of spinach is perfectly complemented by mellow sweet potato in this dish.

SERVES 4–6

4 tablespoons sunflower oil or vegetable oil
1 medium onion, finely sliced
1 teaspoon Five-Spice Mix (see page 13)
2 garlic cloves, crushed
550g (1¼lb) sweet potatoes, cut into 1cm (½in) cubes
1 teaspoon Vegetable and Poultry Spice Blend (see page 14)
1 teaspoon salt or to taste
340g (12oz) frozen spinach, chopped
200ml (7fl oz) Butter Sauce (see page 18)

- Heat half the oil in a small pan and fry the onion for 10–12 minutes, until well browned. Drain on kitchen paper and set aside.

- Meanwhile, heat the remaining oil in a separate pan over medium heat and add the five-spice mix followed by the garlic. Fry over low heat for 30–35 seconds, then add the sweet potatoes, vegetable and poultry spice blend and salt. Stir-fry over medium-high heat until the potatoes are lightly browned.

- Stir in the spinach and butter sauce. Cover the pan and cook over low heat for 10–12 minutes or until the potatoes are tender. Remove the lid and cook for a few minutes until all the liquid has evaporated.

- Stir in the fried onions and remove from the heat. Serve with any meat, poultry or pulse dish.

COOK'S TIP
Thaw the spinach slightly in the microwave for about 3 minutes; then it is easier to chop.

CAULIFLOWER AND POTATOES WITH AROMATIC SPICES

Gobi aloo (cauliflower with potato) is a long-standing favourite side dish and this quick, tasty version is real winner.

SERVES 4

450g (1lb) potatoes, cut into 2.5cm (1in) cubes
3 tablespoons sunflower oil or soya oil
$^1/_2$ teaspoon black mustard seeds
$^1/_2$ teaspoon cumin seeds
4 large garlic cloves, crushed
1–2 green chillies, seeded if liked, chopped

280g (10oz) cauliflower
$^3/_4$ teaspoon salt or to taste
2 teaspoons Vegetable and Poultry Spice Blend (see page 14)
2–3 tablespoons chopped fresh coriander leaves

- Boil the potatoes until almost tender, drain and refresh in cold water.

- Heat the oil in a frying pan over medium heat and add the mustard followed by the cumin seeds. When the seeds begin to crackle, reduce the heat to low and add the garlic and chillies. Fry gently until the garlic begins to brown.

- Add the cauliflower and salt, and sprinkle 3 tablespoons water over the vegetables. Stir once, cover the pan and cook for 9–10 minutes, stirring and rearranging the vegetables at least twice.

- Add the potatoes and the vegetable and poultry spice blend. Increase the heat to medium-high and cook for 2–3 minutes, stirring continuously. Stir in the coriander leaves, remove from the heat and serve.

SWEETCORN IN SUNFLOWER AND COCONUT SAUCE

Swaying fields of corn are a sight to behold throughout the northern Indian state of Punjab. In this recipe, a southern touch is used to cook the produce of the north.

SERVES 4–6

4 tablespoons sunflower oil
½ teaspoon black mustard seeds
½ teaspoon cumin seeds
1 large onion, finely chopped
1–2 green chillies, seeded if liked, finely chopped
½ teaspoon ground turmeric
30g (1oz) sunflower seeds

30g (1oz) desiccated coconut
400g (14oz) frozen sweetcorn kernels
1 courgette, cut into small cubes
1 teaspoon salt or to taste
90ml (3fl oz) warm water
2 tablespoons chopped fresh coriander leaves

- Heat the oil over medium heat and add the mustard seeds. As soon as they pop, add the cumin, followed by the onion and chillies. Fry for 9–10 minutes, until the onions are soft and lightly browned, then add the turmeric.

- Meanwhile, grind the sunflower seeds in a coffee mill until almost fine, then add the coconut and continue to grind until the mixture is fine. Add the ground mixture to the onions and fry for 1 minute.

- Add the sweetcorn, courgette and salt. Stir and pour in the water. Reduce the heat to low, cover the pan and cook for 5–6 minutes.

- Stir in the coriander leaves. Serve with any meat, poultry or egg curry and chapatis.

PEAS IN COCONUT AND ROASTED CUMIN SAUCE

Cumin, garlic and chillies create the perfect background for sweet-tasting peas in a dish that will add a special zest to the plainest meal.

SERVES 4–6

2 tablespoons sunflower oil or vegetable oil
1 teaspoon cumin seeds
1 teaspoon crushed dried chillies
2–3 garlic cloves, crushed
450g (1lb) frozen peas

³/₄ teaspoon salt or to taste
2 tablespoons desiccated coconut
¹/₂ teaspoon Ground Roasted Cumin (see page 13)
1 tablespoon lemon juice

- Heat the oil in a saucepan over low heat. Add the cumin, followed by the chilli flakes, then the garlic, and fry gently for 1 minute.

- Add the peas and salt, sprinkle in 2–3 tablespoons water and cover the pan. Cook over low heat for 8–10 minutes.

- Meanwhile, coarsely grind the coconut in a coffee mill or use a mortar and pestle as it does not have to be very fine, then add it to the peas along with the roasted cumin and lemon juice. Stir over medium heat for 1–2 minutes before serving.

BRAISED CABBAGE WITH MUSTARD AND FENUGREEK

Although used in small quantities, mustard and fenugreek stand out as the main flavours in this recipe. Green cabbage is the best – wash it after you have chopped it and use it straight away, with some of the water still clinging to the chopped leaves.

SERVES 4–5

2 tablespoons sunflower oil or soya oil, plus 2 teaspoons
$\frac{1}{2}$ teaspoon black mustard seeds
$\frac{1}{2}$ teaspoon cumin seeds
1 green cabbage, trimmed and finely chopped
$\frac{1}{2}$ teaspoon ground turmeric

1 teaspoon salt or to taste
2–4 dried red chillies, snipped into small pieces
6–8 fenugreek seeds
1 tablespoon desiccated coconut
1 tablespoon lemon juice

- Heat the 2 tablespoons oil in a saucepan. When hot, but not smoking, add the mustard seeds, then as soon as they start popping, add the cumin followed by the cabbage, turmeric and salt. Sprinkle in 2–3 tablespoons water, stir and mix thoroughly. Cover the pan and cook over low heat for 12–15 minutes or until the cabbage is tender but still firm.

- Meanwhile, heat the 2 teaspoons oil in a small saucepan over low heat. Fry the dried red chillies and the fenugreek seeds until they are just a shade darker, but not dark brown. Add the coconut and stir until the coconut is lightly browned.

- Transfer the coconut and spice mixture to a mortar and grind it with a pestle or process in a coffee mill until finely ground. Add the ground mixture to the cabbage with the lemon juice and stir over medium heat for about 1 minute. Serve at once.

CHUNKY TOMATOES IN MELLOW COCONUT SAUCE

In this simple but exquisite recipe, the only point on which to take particular care is to let the onion cook gently until medium-brown.

SERVES 4

3 tablespoons sunflower oil or vegetable oil
½ teaspoon black mustard seeds
1 large onion, separated and finely sliced
1–2 green chillies, seeded if liked, finely chopped
1 teaspoon salt or to taste

450g (1lb) tomatoes
½ teaspoon ground turmeric
½–1 teaspoon chilli powder
1 teaspoon sugar
2 tablespoons desiccated coconut
115g (4oz) frozen peas or cooked fresh peas

- Heat the oil until hot, but not smoking. Add the mustard seeds, then as soon as they start popping add the onion and the chillies. Fry the onions for 8–9 minutes, stirring regularly, then add the salt. The salt will draw out the remaining moisture from the onion allowing it to brown to the required shade. Reduce the heat slightly, if necessary, and continue to fry for a further 4–5 minutes.

- While the onions are cooking, put the tomatoes in a large heatproof bowl and pour in boiling water to cover them. Leave the tomatoes to stand for 1 minute, then drain and refresh with cold water. Peel away the skin and halve or quarter the tomatoes according to size.

- Stir the turmeric and chilli powder into the onions, then add the tomatoes. Add the sugar, stir and cover the pan. Cook over low to medium heat for 6–8 minutes.

- Meanwhile, grind the coconut in a coffee mill or mortar and pestle, and add to the tomatoes along with the peas. Cook, covered, for 10–12 minutes. Remove from the heat and serve with rice or bread.

CARROTS IN SPICY SPLIT-PEA SAUCE

Small cubes of carrot combined with a mixture of ground spices, split peas and coconut have a striking appearance as well as a fabulous flavour.

SERVES 4

2 tablespoons sunflower oil or vegetable oil plus 2 teaspoons
3/4 teaspoon black mustard seeds
450g (1lb) carrots, peeled and cut into 5mm (1/4in) cubes
3/4 teaspoon salt or to taste
1/2 teaspoon sugar
1/2–1 teaspoon chilli powder

90ml (3fl oz) water
2 teaspoons coriander seeds
1 tablespoon channa dhal or yellow split peas
1/2 teaspoon fenugreek seeds
1 tablespoon desiccated coconut
2 tablespoons snipped fresh chives
1 tablespoon lemon juice

- Heat the two tablespoons oil in a saucepan and add the mustard seeds. As soon as they start popping, add the carrots, salt, sugar and chilli powder. Stir over medium heat for 2–3 minutes, then pour in the water. Reduce the heat slightly, cover the pan and cook for 10–12 minutes, until the carrots are tender, but still firm.

- Meanwhile, heat the 2 teaspoons oil in a small pan over gentle heat and add the coriander seeds and channa dhal or yellow split peas. Fry gently for about 1 minute or until the dhal are lightly browned, but take care not to let them darken any more than this. Add the fenugreek seeds and fry for 15–20 seconds, then remove from the heat.

- Cool the dhal mixture for a few minutes, then grind it with the coconut in a coffee mill until smooth. The oil used for frying and the natural oil present in the coconut will cause the mixture to stick to the blades, but simply scrape it off occasionally and continue grinding.

- Add the ground mixture to the carrots and stir over medium heat until all the liquid is absorbed. Stir in the chives and lemon juice and serve.

ROASTED SPICED AUBERGINES

Traditionally the spiced aubergines are deep-fried, but because aubergines soak up oil like a sponge, I have roasted them with just a sprinkling of sunflower oil. When cooked, they are soft, seductive and thoroughly delicious.

SERVES 4

2 large aubergines, about 450g (1lb)
2–3 tablespoons sunflower oil
½ teaspoon ground turmeric
½ teaspoon chilli powder

½ Ground Roasted Coriander (see page 13)
½ teaspoon Ground Roasted Cumin (see page 13)
½ teaspoon salt or to taste

- Preheat the oven to 220°C/425°F/Gas 7.

- Quarter the aubergines lengthways and cut them into 5cm (2in) pieces, then place in a roasting tin. Sprinkle the oil, spices and salt evenly over the aubergine, then mix them in thoroughly with your fingertips.

- Roast the aubergines in the centre of the oven for 12–14 minutes, until tender and browned in places. Serve hot.

DEEP-FRIED SPICED OKRA

Okra is full of essential nutrients, such as calcium, potassium and vitamin C. Crisp fried and spiced, it is simply divine with any Indian meal.

SERVES 4

400g (14oz) okra
1 large onion, about 200g (7oz), halved and sliced
30g (1oz) polenta or cornmeal
30g (1oz) besan (gram or chick-pea flour), sifted
2 teaspoons Ground Roasted Coriander (see page 13)

2 teaspoons Ground Roasted Cumin (see page 13)
1–1$\frac{1}{2}$ teaspoons chilli powder
$\frac{1}{2}$ teaspoon ground turmeric
1 teaspoon salt or to taste
sunflower oil for frying

- Gently scrub the okra, then trim off their tops and tail ends. Slice each pod diagonally into 3–4 pieces according to size. Separate the onion slices into half-rings.

- In a large mixing bowl, mix the remaining ingredients. Add the okra and onion, and work them gently into the spiced mixture with your fingertips. Do not be tempted to add water – the mixture should be dry, but it will stick to the moist vegetables if you mix the ingredients with your fingers rather than a spoon.

- Pour enough oil into a frying pan to give a depth of about 2.5cm (1in) and place over high heat. When the oil is very hot, but not smoking, fry the okra mixture in batches until crisp and golden brown. Do not overcrowd the pan as this will lower the temperature of the oil too much, resulting in soggy vegetables.

- Drain the okra on kitchen paper and serve immediately.

CHILLI, LIME AND CORIANDER CHICK PEAS

This simple dish is amazingly tasty as a side dish, or on small savoury biscuits as a snack, or on hot buttered toast as a light meal. The quantities given are for a side dish, and are enough for two portions if the chick peas are served as a light meal.

SERVES 4

400g (14oz) can chick peas, drained and rinsed
55g (2oz) butter
1 large red onion, finely chopped
2.5cm (1in) piece cinnamon stick
4 cloves

2 bay leaves, crumpled
1–1½ teaspoon chilli powder
¼ teaspoon salt or to taste
15g (½oz) fresh coriander leaves and stalks, finely chopped
1 tablespoon lime juice

- Lightly mash the chick peas with a fork.

- Melt the butter over low heat and add the onion, cinnamon, cloves and bay leaves. Fry for 8–9 minutes, until the onion is soft and lightly browned.

- Add the chick peas, chilli powder and salt. Stir until the chick peas are heated through, then add the coriander leaves. Cook for about 1 minute, stir in the lime juice and serve hot, or leave to cool and serve on savoury biscuits.

Breads, Chutneys & Raitas

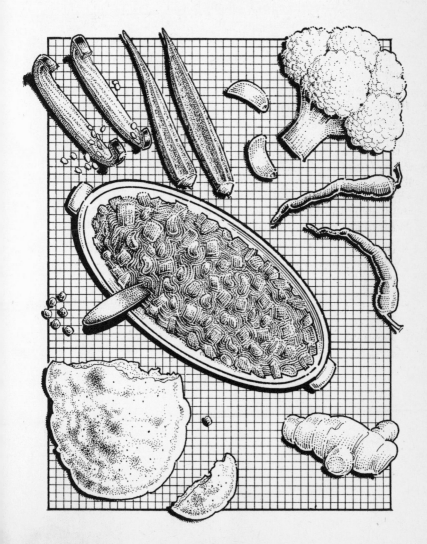

Indian breads are usually made using wholewheat flour (*atta*). While flat griddle-roasted breads, such as chapatis and parathas, are for everyday eating, leavened breads are served on special occasions and for celebration meals.

Making Indian breads can be time-consuming, but they do freeze well, so I have included a few different recipes in this section so that you can stock up when you have time to spare. You may succumb to buying from the huge variety of breads sold in the supermarkets; with a little imagination, they can be greatly enhanced – for example, try Khurmi Naan (see page 167). Simply brushing plain naan or pitta breads with a little melted butter, then sprinkling with caraway, poppy or sesame seeds and grilling them until hot, gives deliciously different results. Instead of the seeds, you can use fresh herbs such as coriander, mint and chives.

Chutneys and raitas always add an extra dimension to Indian meals. I hope you will be delighted with, and inspired by, the varied and simple chutneys and raitas in this chapter, including Rhubarb Chutney with Roasted Cumin (see page 170) and Fresh Plum Chutney (see page 172). Broccoli and Red Pepper Raita (see page 174) and Potato and Pomegranate Raita (see page 179) are welcome alternatives to the familiar cucumber raita. Pickles are the other traditional condiment, but making them is an art demanding care, attention and time, so I included just one, Prawn Balchao (see page 168), as it is relatively easy to make. Good-quality commercial pickles are readily available, so you can buy them with confidence.

WHOLEWHEAT PANCAKES

These pancakes are easy to make and delicious with dry or semi-dry dishes. I enjoy them served as egg rolls – filled with omelette cut into strips and rolled up. The batter is made without eggs, using chapati flour (*atta*) for a wholesome flavour. Wholemeal flour can be used, but avoid using strong flour.

MAKES 6

175g (6oz) chapati flour
55g (2oz) semolina
½ teaspoon salt or to taste
2 tablespoons plain yogurt
500ml (17fl oz) water

2–3 green chillies, seeded if liked, finely chopped
2 tablespoons finely chopped fresh coriander leaves
oil for shallow frying

- Mix the flour, semolina, salt, yogurt and water together to make a smooth batter. Add the chillies and coriander leaves and mix well. Measure 120ml (4fl oz) of the batter into a jug.

- Heat a cast-iron griddle or heavy frying pan (preferably non-stick) over medium heat and add 1 tablespoon oil. Spread the oil quickly over the entire surface and wait until it is at smoking point.

- Pour the batter from the jug on to the pan, then spread it evenly with the back of metal spoon, filling any gaps or holes. Cook for 30–40 seconds, then sprinkle about 1 tablespoon water around the edge. Cook for a further 30–40 seconds, then turn the pancake. Do this carefully, by first loosening the pancake all around the edge using a thin spatula or a fish slice.

- Cook until both sides are browned, allowing a total cooking time of about 2½–3 minutes. Transfer to a wire rack to cool; if the pancakes are stacked or placed on a solid surface they become soggy. Repeat with the remaining batter.

COOK'S TIP
The first pancake may not be successful (it often looks like scrambled egg when I make these), but once the pan is well-heated to a stable temperature and oiled, the remaining pancakes will be fine.

BASIC CHAPATIS

Chapatis, the daily bread, are not difficult to make using a food mixer or processor and they freeze very well. This basic recipe can be transformed into special breads, as you will see in the recipes that follow, or flavoured with a sprinkling of herbs or spices.

MAKES 16

400g (14oz) chapati flour (*atta*)
½–1 teaspoon salt or to taste
2–3 tablespoons sunflower oil or
  vegetable oil

250ml (8½fl oz) lukewarm water

- If you are using a food mixer, start by blending the salt and flour together, then add the oil and water. Knead the dough until it is smooth, then cover with a damp cloth and set aside for 20–30 minutes.

- If mixing by hand, put the flour in a large mixing bowl, add the salt and work it in with your fingertips. Add the oil and work it into the flour well, then gradually add the water. Mix until a soft, slightly sticky dough is formed. Knead the dough for 4–5 minutes, until it is smooth and no longer sticky. Cover and set aside as above.

- Divide the dough in half and shape 8 equal-sized balls from each half. Flatten the balls of dough into small round cakes and work on one portion at a time, keeping the remaining cakes covered. Dust a portion of dough lightly with flour and roll it out into a 15cm (6in) circle. Repeat with the remaining dough.

- Preheat a heavy cast-iron griddle or frying pan over medium-high heat. Place a chapati on the griddle and cook until bubbles begin to appear on the surface. Use a fish slice to turn the chapati, then cook until the underneath is speckled with brown patches. Gently lift the edge of the chapati to check the cooking progress.

- Turn the chapati again and press the edges down to encourage the middle to puff up. Cook until the underneath is also speckled with brown patches. Remove and wrap in foil lined with a clean tea-towel or kitchen paper to keep hot until you finish cooking the remaining dough.

- Once the pan is well heated, you may need to turn the heat down slightly to prevent the breads from being cooked too quickly.

COOK'S TIP
To freeze the chapatis, cool them on a wire rack as they are cooked instead of keeping them hot. Leave them until completely cool, then layer sheets of freezer film between them and pack in a freezer bag.

FENUGREEK AND CHILLI CHAPATIS

When making a large batch of flavoured chapatis for freezing, remember to make a note on the label of the herbs and/or spices used to flavour the dough.

MAKES 16

1 quantity Basic Chapatis (see page 162)
2 tablespoons dried fenugreek leaves

½–1 teaspoon chilli powder
sunflower oil or vegetable oil for cooking or butter for serving

- Follow the instructions for making the chapatis, adding the fenugreek leaves and chilli powder to the flour and salt before mixing in the oil and water. Finish making, resting and shaping the dough as in the basic recipe.

- When cooking the chapatis, spread a little oil (about 1 teaspoon) around the edges of the breads. Alternatively, spread a little butter on the freshly cooked chapatis – just like buttering a piece of toast.

MINT AND CORIANDER CHAPATIS

Mint and coriander are a classic, refreshing combination.

MAKES 16

1 quantity Basic Chapatis (see page 162)

2 tablespoons finely chopped fresh mint or 1 teaspoon dried mint

3 tablespoons finely chopped fresh coriander leaves

freshly ground black pepper

sunflower oil or vegetable oil for cooking or butter for serving

---

- Follow the instructions for making the chapatis, adding the mint, coriander and pepper to the flour and salt before mixing in the oil and water. Finish making, resting and shaping the dough as in the basic recipe.

- When cooking the chapatis, spread a little oil (about 1 teaspoon) around the edges of the breads. Alternatively, spread a little butter on the freshly cooked chapatis – just like buttering a piece of toast.

EASY NAAN

Although traditional recipes for naan are not as difficult as they may seem, once you have tried this totally simplified version you will never go back to the original. The dough can be made in a food processor.

MAKES 8

450g (1lb) self-raising flour
1 teaspoon baking powder
1 teaspoon salt or to taste
2 teaspoons sugar

55g (2oz) softened butter
250ml (8½fl oz) lukewarm milk
melted butter for brushing

- Sift the flour, baking powder, salt and sugar into a bowl. Rub in the butter, then gradually mix in the milk. Knead the dough for at least 5 minutes, then cover with a damp cloth and leave to rest for 20–30 minutes.

- Preheat the grill to high for 8–10 minutes. Line a grill pan with foil and grease it well.

- Divide the dough into 8 equal portions. Roll out a portion of dough into a circle measuring about 12cm (5in) in diameter. Gently pull one edge to form a tear-drop shape, then roll out to about 23cm (9in), maintaining the tear-drop shape. Repeat with the remaining dough.

- Grill the naan in batches about 12cm (5in) below the heat source for 1½ minutes. As they puff up, the naan rise closer to the heat source and are likely to burn easily, so watch them closely. Turn and grill for about 1 minute or until brown patches appear on the second side.

- Place on a clean tea-towel and brush with a little butter. Wrap in the towel to keep hot until all the breads are cooked.

COOK'S TIP
The cooled naan can be frozen. Thaw and reheat in a toaster on the minimum setting or moisten both sides with water and reheat under a preheated grill, turning once, until the surface is dry.

KHURMI NAAN

These pizza-style naan are ready in a few minutes. They are great for picnics and snack lunches. If you do not have plain naan in the freezer, use pitta bread. Most of the naan sold in supermarkets tend to be flavoured, so you may have to rely on your stock of frozen home-made breads.

MAKES 12

12 plain naan or plain or wholemeal pitta breads
1 tablespoon plain yogurt
115g (4oz) red Leicester or Cheddar cheese, grated

2 tomatoes, chopped
2–3 green chillies, seeded and chopped
2 tablespoons chopped fresh coriander leaves

- Preheat the grill and line a grill pan with foil. Grease the foil.

- Hold each bread under cold running water for 5–10 seconds, then shake off excess water and place in the prepared pan. Grill the first side only until the surface water dries up, then turn the breads.

- Brush the breads with yogurt. Mix the remaining ingredients and spread evenly over the breads. Grill until the cheese begins to bubble. Cut into strips and serve hot or cold.

PRAWN BALCHAO

Portuguese influence gives this Goan pickle its particular character. Although the pickle can be eaten freshly made, it tastes infinitely better when matured for 3–4 weeks. Stored correctly in a moisture-free, sterilized jar, the pickle will keep for 6 months.

MAKES 450G (1LB)

400g (14oz) uncooked prawns, peeled
1½ teaspoons coarse salt or to taste
150ml (5fl oz) sunflower oil
1 teaspoon black mustard seeds
2 teaspoons ground turmeric
½ teaspoon asafoetida
1–3 teaspoons chilli powder

10–12 large garlic cloves, minced or crushed to a pulp
5cm (2in) cube fresh root ginger, peeled and finely grated
2 teaspoons Ground Roasted Cumin (see page 13)
150ml (5fl oz) cider vinegar

- Mix the prawns thoroughly with 1 teaspoon of the salt and then tie them up in a piece of muslin. Place it in a sieve over a bowl and put a weight on top. Leave to drain for about 1 hour.

- Heat the oil in a saucepan until smoking point, then reduce the heat to low. Add the mustard seeds, then the turmeric and asafoetida. Follow on quickly with the prawns and increase the heat to high. Fry the prawns for 4–5 minutes.

- Add the remaining salt, chilli powder, garlic, ginger and cumin. Reduce the heat to medium and fry the ingredients until all the moisture evaporates and the oil begins to float on the surface.

- Pour in the vinegar and remove from the heat. Cool thoroughly and store in a sterilized airtight jar in a cool dry place. Serve with any bread or rice and dhal.

COOK'S TIP
Asafoetida is an essential ingredient in this pickle. You can buy it from Indian stores in block or ground form. Blocks are better as they retain more flavour than the powder. Grate enough spice off the block of asafoetida as required. Asafoetida is used in minute quantities as it has a strong flavour.

MINT AND YOGURT CHUTNEY

The aroma of mint and coriander combined with their fresh flavours lifts the plainest dishes to new heights. This chutney can be served instead of a raita, or spooned on to mini pappadums as a snack, or used as a superb dressing for boiled new potatoes. It will keep for 4–5 days in the refrigerator.

SERVES 4–6

2 tablespoons sunflower oil
2 red onions, about 250g (9oz), roughly chopped
85g (3oz) plain yogurt
115g (4oz) fresh mint leaves
2–3 tablespoons roughly chopped fresh oriander leaves

1–2 green chillies, seeded if liked, chopped
$\frac{1}{2}$ teaspoon salt or to taste
$\frac{1}{2}$ teaspoon sugar
1 tablespoon lemon juice

- Heat the oil over medium heat and fry the onions for 5–6 minutes, until soft, but not brown.

- Put the yogurt in a blender and add the fried onion along with the remaining ingredients. Add 3–4 tablespoons water and blend until smooth. The chutney can be served at room temperature or chilled.

RHUBARB CHUTNEY WITH ROASTED CUMIN

An amalgamation of exciting flavours makes this chutney a real taste-bud reviver. It is excellent with all kinds of fried snacks.

SERVES 4–6

1kg (2¼lb) rhubarb
4 tablespoons sunflower oil
½ teaspoon mustard seeds
1 teaspoon Five-Spice Mix (see page 13)
2.5cm (1in) cube fresh root ginger, peeled and grated, or 2 teaspoons Ginger Purée (see page 16)

1–3 teaspoons chilli powder
2 teaspoons Ground Roasted Cumin (see page 13)
1 teaspoon salt or to taste
115–140g (4–5oz) soft brown sugar
55g (2oz) seedless raisins

• Peel the rhubarb if it is old or coarse and stringy. Young rhubarb will not need peeling. Then cut it into 1cm (½in) pieces.

• Heat the oil over low heat. Add the mustard seeds, then the five-spice mix. Let the seeds crackle for 15–20 seconds before adding the ginger. Cook gently for 1 minute, then add the chilli powder and cumin, immediately followed by the rhubarb, salt and sugar.

• Stir over medium heat for 2–3 minutes, then reduce the heat to low again. Cover the pan with a piece of moist greaseproof paper, then with a lid, and cook for 8–10 minutes.

• Discard the greaseproof paper and add the raisins. Cook, uncovered, over low heat for 12–15 minutes, stirring occasionally, until thickened.

• Leave the chutney to cool completely, then store it in a perfectly clean and dry airtight jar in the refrigerator. In this way, it will keep well for up to 2 weeks.

PINEAPPLE CHUTNEY

Succulent pineapple, cashew nuts and raisins are seasoned with a classic mix of East Indian spices in this superb chutney. You can vary the result by using dried dates instead of the raisins and/or dried apricots or peaches instead of the cashew nuts.

MAKES 340G (12OZ)

- 1 small ripe, firm pineapple
- 3 tablespoons sunflower oil or vegetable oil
- 1 teaspoon Five-Spice Mix (see page 13)
- 1½ teaspoons Ground Roasted Cumin (see page 13)
- 1 teaspoon Ground Roasted Coriander (see page 13)
- 1–3 teaspoons chilli powder
- 30g (1oz) seedless raisins
- 55g (2oz) unsalted cashew nuts
- 1 teaspoon ground ginger
- 1½ teaspoons salt or to taste
- 115g (4oz) soft brown sugar
- 1 tablespoon white wine vinegar or cider vinegar

- Quarter the pineapple lengthways, peel it and remove the spines, if necessary with a small sharp knife. Remove the central core and cut the flesh into fairly small chunks.

- Heat the oil in a saucepan over medium heat and add the five-spice mix followed by the cumin, coriander and chilli powder.

- Add the pineapple with all the remaining ingredients, except the vinegar, stir and reduce the heat to low. Cover the pan and cook gently for 45–50 minutes, stirring occasionally.

- Stir in the vinegar and remove from the heat. The pineapple should be cooked, but in small soft chunks. When the chutney is cold, transfer it to a sterilized airtight jar. It will keep well in a cool place for 4–5 weeks.

FRESH PLUM CHUTNEY

Choose ripe but firm plums for this recipe, in which delicate sweet and sour flavours are intensified with overtones of chilli and aromatic spices. I cannot think of a better accompaniment to lamb and turkey dishes. Besides enjoying the chutney with Indian meals, serve it with plain grilled or roast lamb, turkey or pork.

MAKES ABOUT 225G (8OZ)

3 tablespoons sunflower oil or vegetable oil
1/2 teaspoon black mustard seeds
1/2 teaspoon onion seeds
675g (1 1/2lb) firm ripe plums, stoned and cut into small chunks
1 teaspoons chilli powder

1 teaspoon salt or to taste
85g (3oz) sugar
1 teaspoon cumin seeds
1 teaspoon fennel seeds
1/4 teaspoon fenugreek seeds
2–3 dried red chillies, chopped

- Reserve 1 tablespoon oil and heat the remainder in a heavy-based saucepan over medium heat. Add the mustard seeds, then, as soon as they start crackling, add the onion seeds followed by the plums.

- Add the chilli powder, salt and sugar. Stir until the mixture begins to bubble, then reduce the heat to low or medium and simmer, uncovered, for 15 minutes.

- Meanwhile, heat the remaining oil in a small pan over low heat. Fry the cumin and fennel seeds for 25–30 seconds. Add the fenugreek seeds and chillies and fry for a further 15–20 seconds. Remove from the heat and crush the spice mixture with a pestle or rolling pin.

- Add the crushed mixture to the chutney and cook for 5–7 minutes, stirring regularly to ensure that the thickened chutney does not stick to the bottom of the pan. Cool and store in a sterilized jar in the refrigerator for up to 2 weeks.

APPLE AND COCONUT CHUTNEY

The soft green appearance of this chutney matches its delicate flavour amazingly well. It is good with a plain piece of toast or a savoury biscuit as well as with spicy snacks, such as Prawn Koftas (see page 36) or Courgette Bhajiyas (see page 45).

SERVES 4–5

85g (3oz) freshly grated coconut
1 dessert apple, such as Granny Smith, cored
15g (½oz) fresh coriander leaves and stalks, roughly chopped
5mm (¼in) cube fresh root ginger, chopped

1 garlic clove, chopped
¾ teaspoon salt or to taste
½ teaspoon sugar
1 tablespoon lemon juice
175ml (6fl oz) cold water

- Put all the ingredients in a food processor or blender and process until smooth.

- Transfer to a serving dish. Serve at room temperature or lightly chilled.

COOK'S TIP
Desiccated coconut can be used instead of fresh coconut. Use 55g (2oz) desiccated coconut and soak it in 175ml (6fl oz) boiling water for 10–15 minutes, then blend with the soaking water instead of the cold water.

BROCCOLI AND RED PEPPER RAITA

Colourful broccoli and red pepper make an attractive raita with yogurt and the flavour combination is excellent.

SERVES 4

2 tablespoons sunflower oil or vegetable oil
$1/2$ teaspoon black mustard seeds
$1/2$ teaspoon cumin seeds
$1/2$ teaspoon crushed dried chillies
85g (3oz) bite-sized broccoli florets

1 small or $1/2$ large red pepper, seeded and cut into bite-sized pieces
$1/4$ teaspoon salt or to taste
225g (8oz) plain mild yogurt

- Heat the oil over medium heat in a small saucepan. When hot, but not smoking, add the mustard seeds. As soon as they crackle, add the cumin followed by the crushed chillies.

- Add the broccoli, peppers and salt. Stir, cover the pan and cook over gentle heat for 3–4 minutes. Remove from the heat and allow to cool.

- Beat the yogurt until smooth and stir in the cooled vegetables. Serve chilled or at room temperature.

TOMATO RAITA

This is a popular raita from the Karnataka district of southern India. Freshly grated or desiccated coconut adds richness, but it can be omitted if you want to limit the fat content. Try scattering a tablespoon of toasted pine nuts over the raita for a tasty alternative.

SERVES 4

225g (8oz) plain mild yogurt
30g (1oz) desiccated coconut
½ teaspoon salt or to taste
½ teaspoon sugar
340g (12oz) firm ripe tomatoes, cut into bite-sized pieces
1 tablespoon lemon juice

2 teaspoons sunflower oil or vegetable oil
½ teaspoon black mustard seeds
½ teaspoon cumin seeds
1 green chilli, seeded if liked, finely chopped

- Put the yogurt in a mixing bowl and beat with a fork or wire beater until smooth.

- Grind the coconut in a mortar with a pestle, or in a coffee mill, until smooth, then mix with the yogurt. Stir in the salt, sugar, tomatoes and lemon juice.

- Heat the oil in a small saucepan over medium heat. When hot, but not smoking, throw in the mustard seeds. As soon as they pop, add the cumin followed by the chillies. Fry for 15–20 seconds, then pour the spices over the raita. Mix and serve.

RADISH RAITA

Radishes are low in calories and high in vitamins and minerals. The hot oil seasoning enhances the flavour of radish and yogurt, and gives this raita an interesting appearance.

SERVES 4

225g (8oz) plain yogurt
½ teaspoon salt or to taste
½ teaspoon sugar
2 bunches small red radishes, about 250g (9oz), sliced
2 teaspoons sunflower oil

½ teaspoon black mustard seeds
1 green chilli, seeded if liked, chopped
6–8 fresh curry leaves or 10–12 dried curry leaves

- Beat the yogurt until smooth and add the salt, sugar and radishes. Mix and set aside.

- Heat the oil in a small pan over gentle heat. When hot, switch off the heat and add the mustard seeds. As soon as they pop, add the chilli and curry leaves. Let the spices sizzle for 15–20 seconds, then pour them over the raita. Mix and serve.

ONION RAITA WITH ROASTED PEANUTS

Onions are often eaten with Indian meals. They are usually served dressed with a squeeze of lemon, fresh chillies and salt. Finely chopped red onions with roasted peanuts and a touch of spice make a sensational relish.

SERVES 4–6

175g (6oz) plain mild yogurt
1 small garlic clove
1 small green chilli, seeded if liked, chopped
1/4 teaspoon salt or to taste
1/2 teaspoon sugar

85g (3oz) roasted salted peanuts
1 red onion, finely chopped
1/4 teaspoon Ground Roasted Cumin (see page 13)
1/4 teaspoon chilli powder or paprika

- Put the yogurt in a mixing bowl and whisk until smooth. Using a mortar and pestle, crush the garlic, chilli, salt and sugar together to a paste, and stir this into the yogurt.

- Put the peanuts in a plastic bag and crush them lightly with a pestle or rolling pin, then add to the yogurt. Stir in the onion.

- Mix the raita thoroughly and transfer it to a serving dish. Sprinkle the roasted cumin and chilli powder or paprika on top.

WHITE RADISH AND CARROT RAITA

Crunchy white radish and carrot combine with thick, creamy yogurt to make a deliciously healthy side dish. A dressing of flavoured oil enlivens the familiar flavours and appearance of this raita.

SERVES 4

225g (8oz) plain mild yogurt
225g (8oz) white radish, grated
115g (4oz) carrots, grated
1 tablespoon sunflower oil
$\frac{1}{2}$ teaspoon black mustard seeds
$\frac{1}{2}$ teaspoon black peppercorns, lightly crushed
$\frac{1}{2}$ teaspoon cumin seeds, lightly crushed
$\frac{1}{2}$ teaspoon salt or to taste
1 tablespoon chopped fresh coriander leaves
$\frac{1}{4}$ teaspoon paprika or chilli powder

- Pour the yogurt into a mixing bowl and beat until smooth. Add the radish and carrots, mix well and set aside.

- Heat the oil in a small pan over medium heat, then add the mustard seeds. As soon as the seeds begin to crackle, switch off the heat and add the pepper and cumin. Cook the spices in the heat remaining in the oil for 15–20 seconds, then pour the spiced oil over the raita.

- Add the salt and coriander leaves. Transfer to a serving dish and serve sprinkled with the paprika or chilli powder.

POTATO AND POMEGRANATE RAITA

This simple dish is likely to be the star rather than a supporting member of the menu! Cumin and chilli provide warm bursts of flavour in the cool, creamy yogurt, and the pomegranate seeds bring a luxurious, delicately sweet-sour flavour along with their crunchy texture.

SERVES 4–5

225g (8oz) potatoes, cut into 1cm (½in) cubes
2 tablespoons sunflower oil or vegetable oil
¼ teaspoon fennel seeds
1 large garlic clove, crushed

½ teaspoon salt or to taste
½ teaspoon Ground Roasted Cumin (see page 13)
¼ teaspoon chilli powder
1 small pomegranate
200g (7oz) plain mild yogurt

- Wash and drain the potatoes and thoroughly dry them in a clean tea-towel.

- Heat the oil over gentle heat in a non-stick frying pan and fry the fennel and garlic gently until the garlic is light brown.

- Add the potatoes and salt, stir over medium heat for 2–3 minutes, then cover the pan and reduce the heat slightly. Cook for 8–9 minutes, stirring regularly, until the potatoes are tender and lightly browned.

- Sprinkle the cumin and chilli powder over the potatoes, stir and remove from the heat. Allow to cool completely.

- Meanwhile, peel the pomegranate and remove the seeds, discarding the white membrane. This is like peeling an orange. Reserve half the seeds for this dish. The remainder can be used in a salad, to garnish a pilau or on Saffron Rice (see page 194). They are also delicious scattered on plain yogurt as a dessert.

- Beat the yogurt in a mixing bowl until smooth. Mix in the cooled potatoes and transfer to a serving dish. Scatter the pomegranate seeds over the top and serve.

Microwave Recipes

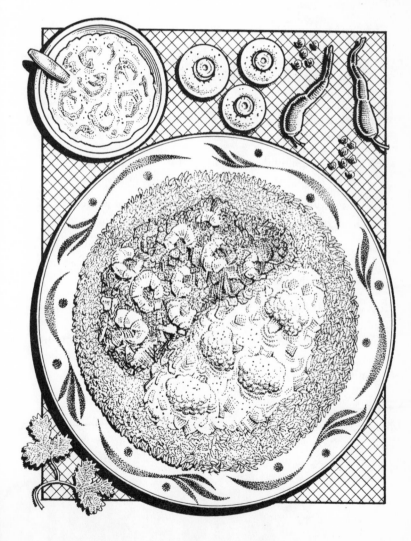

I have included most of the rice recipes in this section. Microwave cooking is one of the simplest methods for rice, especially for those who worry about being able to cook it successfully by conventional methods. You will never be disappointed with the result if you follow the recipes closely. Simply shut the microwave door and forget about it!

Always read and follow the manufacturer's instructions and basic rules for microwave cooking and you will not go wrong when cooking Indian dishes. The following are the main points to remember:

- Cut food into small, even pieces.

- Use the correct cooking dish. Porcelain, china and glass (except lead crystal) without any metal trimmings or decorations are suitable. There is also a large range of specialist microwave cookware.

- Stir food regularly to ensure that the food cooks evenly. Always stir from the sides of the dish towards the centre.

- Use less cooking liquid, as evaporation is minimal in the microwave.

- Cover food during cooking. If using cling film, puncture it or peel it back slightly to allow steam to escape.

- Leave the food to stand before serving. Being extremely hot inside, the food will continue to cook for a while and become even in temperature as hot spots disperse.

- It is often most practical to use the microwave to complement traditional methods. When a traditional recipe reaches its simmering stage, it can be transferred to a suitable container and finished on defrost or simmer setting. Remember to reduce the quantity of liquid used in the recipe.

NOTE
All the recipes in this chapter have been tested in an 850-watt output microwave. Notes on microwave cooking throughout the book are a guide to cooking at this output. Adjust the cooking times according to the capacity of your own oven.

PRAWNS IN COCONUT MILK

In the kitchens of coastal India, large succulent prawns and milk from freshly grated coconut would be used in this recipe. To adapt the recipe for microwave cooking and supermarket shopping, I use peeled uncooked prawns and creamed coconut. I am sure you will be delighted with both the lightning speed at which the dish can be prepared and the superbly flavoured result!

SERVES 4

85g (3oz) creamed coconut
150ml (5fl oz) boiling water
1cm (½in) cube fresh root ginger, peeled and grated, or
  1 teaspoon Ginger Purée (see page 16)
1 green chilli, seeded if liked, sliced at a slant
8–10 fresh curry leaves
1 teaspoon salt or to taste

2 teaspoons Ground Roasted Coriander (see page 13)
1–1½ teaspoons chilli powder
¼ teaspoon ground turmeric
450g (1lb) peeled uncooked prawns
2 small tomatoes, chopped
2 tablespoons sunflower oil
4 large garlic cloves, crushed or minced

- Using the coarse side of a grater, grate the coconut and put it into a 1.2 litre (2 pint) casserole or dish suitable for microwave cooking. Add the boiling water and stir until blended. Add the ginger, green chilli, curry leaves and salt. Cover and cook on high for 1½ minutes.

- Add the coriander, chilli powder and turmeric. Stir the ingredients and add the prawns. Stir until the prawns are coated with the spiced coconut milk. Cover and cook on high for 2 minutes, stir and rearrange the prawns, cover again and cook on medium for 3 minutes.

- Stir in the tomatoes, cover and cook on medium for 2½ minutes. Leave to stand for 5–6 minutes.

- Meanwhile, heat the oil in a small pan over gentle heat on the hob. Fry the garlic for 1–2 minutes, until light brown. Stir the garlic into the prawns and serve with basmati rice or Dill Rice (see page 193).

CHICKEN AND MUSHROOMS IN A HOT TOMATO SAUCE

A microwave browning dish is best for this recipe, but a suitable casserole or a glass bowl of 1.75 litres' (3 pints') capacity can be used instead.

SERVES 4

1 onion
1cm (½in) cube fresh root ginger
2 large garlic cloves
2 tablespoons sunflower oil
2.5cm (1in) piece cinnamon stick
½ teaspoon ground turmeric
1 teaspoon Ground Roasted Coriander (see page 13)
½ teaspoon Ground Roasted Cumin (see page 13)
1–1½ teaspoons chilli powder

2 tablespoons tomato purée
90ml (3fl oz) warm water
675g (1½lb) boneless chicken thighs, halved
1 teaspoon salt or to taste
½ teaspoon sugar
225g (8oz) closed cup mushrooms, thickly sliced
30g (1oz) ground almonds
2 tablespoons finely chopped fresh coriander leaves

- Place the onion, ginger and garlic in a food processor and pulse the power until they are very finely chopped. If you do not have a food processor, finely chop or mince the ingredients.

- Preheat a microwave browning dish on high for 1 minute, or according to the manufacturer's instructions, and add the oil. Heat on high for 1 minute, then add the processed mixture. Add the cinnamon, cover and cook on high for 3 minutes. (If you do not have a browning dish, put the oil and the onion mixture in a casserole or a glass bowl, cover and cook on high for 3 minutes.)

- Stir in the turmeric, coriander, cumin and chilli powder. Cook, uncovered, on medium for 2 minutes. Add the tomato purée and water. Stir until thoroughly mixed, cover and cook on high for 1½ minutes.

- Mix in the chicken, salt and sugar. Cover and cook on high for 4 minutes, stirring halfway through the time. Cook, covered, on medium for 5 minutes, again stirring halfway through.

- Add the mushrooms, stir and cover, then cook on medium for 4 minutes, stirring halfway through the time.

- Finally, add the ground almonds and cook, uncovered, on low for 2 minutes. Stir in the coriander leaves and serve with any bread or basmati rice.

CHICKEN SHAHI KORMA

Shahi korma (meaning royal korma), an age-old recipe from the Indian regal repertoire, can be cooked successfully in the ultra-modern microwave. Traditionally, the chicken is marinated for at least 2 hours, but rubbing lemon juice into it and setting it aside while you assemble the other ingredients is a quick alternative.

SERVES 4

55g (2oz) blanched almonds
150ml (5fl oz) boiling water
675g (1½ lb) boneless chicken breasts, skinned
2 tablespoons lemon juice
1 teaspoon salt
140g (5oz) plain mild yogurt, whisked
30g (1oz) ghee or unsalted butter
1 onion, finely chopped or minced
1cm (½in) cube fresh root ginger, peeled and finely grated, or 1 teaspoon Ginger Purée (see page 16)

2 large garlic cloves, crushed, or 1 teaspoon Garlic Purée (see page 16)
2.5cm (1in) piece cinnamon stick
3 green cardamom pods, bruised
1 tablespoon Ground Roasted Coriander (see page 13)
½ teaspoon freshly grated nutmeg
½ teaspoon freshly ground white pepper
¼ teaspoon ground turmeric
½ teaspoon chilli powder
½ teaspoon sugar
90ml (3fl oz) single cream

- Place the almonds in a bowl and pour in the boiling water, then set aside. Cut the chicken into 2.5cm (1in) cubes. Sprinkle the lemon juice and salt over the chicken, then gently rub the seasoning into the cubes with your fingertips. Add the whisked yogurt, mix thoroughly and set aside.

- Preheat a microwave browning dish for 1–2 minutes on high, or according to the manufacturer's instructions. Add the ghee or butter and heat on medium for 30–40 seconds, until melted.

- Add the onion and cook, uncovered, on high for 5 minutes, stirring halfway through the time. Add the ginger, garlic, cinnamon and cardamoms. Cook on high for 2 minutes, stirring once. Stir in the coriander, nutmeg, pepper, turmeric and chilli powder. Cook on medium for 1 minute.

- Add the chicken with its marinade and the sugar, then stir to mix thoroughly. Cover and cook on high for 4 minutes, stirring halfway through cooking. Then cook on medium for 3 minutes, again stirring halfway through the time. Pour in the cream, cover and cook on medium for $3\frac{1}{2}$ minutes.

- Meanwhile, purée the almonds with the water in which they were soaked. Pour the purée into the chicken mixture. Stir well, cover and cook on medium for 3 minutes, stirring halfway through. Leave to stand for 5–6 minutes before serving with Saffron Rice (see page 194).

COOK'S TIP

If you do not have a browning dish, fry the onion and spices on the hob. Add the chicken and transfer the mixture to a suitable dish, then finish cooking in the microwave as above.

POTATOES IN TAMARIND SAUCE

This tangy, hot potato dish is delicious with chapatis or naan. It also makes a good filling for toasted sandwiches and is good on lightly toasted bread. It is easy to be tempted to cut up the potatoes before boiling, but resist! The potatoes must be neat and dry, not sticky, and this can only be achieved by boiling them in their skins.

SERVES 4

450g (1lb) evenly sized potatoes
240ml (8fl oz) hot water
4 tablespoons sunflower oil
1/2 teaspoon black mustard seeds
1 large onion, finely chopped
2 garlic cloves, roughly chopped

1 teaspoon salt or to taste
1/2–1 1/2 teaspoons chilli powder
1 1/2 teaspoons Ground Roasted Coriander (see page 13)
1 teaspoon tamarind concentrate or 3 tablespoons tamarind juice

- Put the potatoes in a large bowl and add 90ml (3fl oz) of the hot water. Cover and cook on high for 6 minutes, turning the potatoes over after 3 minutes. Leave to stand for 5 minutes, then immerse the potatoes in iced water and leave to cool. (Alternatively, the potatoes can be boiled conventionally and refreshed under cold water, then drained and cooled.)

- While the potatoes are cooling, preheat a microwave browning dish on high for 1 minute, or according to the manufacturer's instructions. Add the oil and heat on high for 1 1/2 minutes. Add the mustard seeds, cover and continue to cook on high for 30 seconds. Add the onion and continue to cook, uncovered, for 5–6 minutes, stirring every minute, until browned.

- If you do not have a browning dish, heat the oil in a saucepan on the hob and add the mustard seeds. When they start popping, add the onion and fry for 10–12 minutes, stirring regularly, until browned.

- Crush the garlic and the salt together and add to the onions. Add the chilli powder and coriander, and cook on high for 30 seconds. Remove and cover the dish. If you are cooking on the hob, the time is the same.

- When the potatoes are cold, peel them and cut into 1cm (½in) cubes. Add them to the spice mix with the tamarind and remaining water. Stir and cook on high for 3 minutes (or for the same time on the hob). The mixture should cling together, looking semi-solid, with the tamarind sauce coating the potatoes.

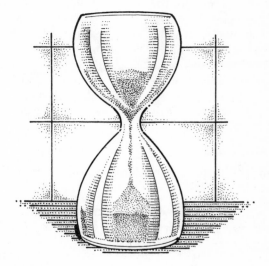

TOMATO AND COCONUT RICE WITH PRAWNS

This simple, speedy and delicious dish makes an exciting and satisfying meal when served with a raita and some pappadums. The rice can be cooked without the prawns to make a versatile side dish to accompany spicy main courses; simply add the tomato and reduce the final cooking time to 1 minute.

SERVES 4

280g (10oz) basmati rice
30g (1oz) coconut milk powder or creamed coconut
600ml (1 pint) boiling water
1 green chilli, seeded and finely chopped
1cm (½in) cube fresh root ginger, peeled and grated, or 1 teaspoon Ginger Purée (see page 16)

1 tablespoon fresh curry leaves or 1½ tablespoons dried curry leaves
¼ teaspoon ground turmeric
1 teaspoon salt or to taste
400g (14oz) peeled cooked prawns, thawed and drained if frozen
1 small tomato, seeded and chopped
1 tablespoon chopped fresh coriander leaves

- Wash the rice in cold water, drain and soak it in fresh cold water for 15 minutes.

- Stir the coconut milk powder into the boiling water. If using creamed coconut, grate it on the coarse blade of a grater before stirring it into the water.

- Drain the rice and put into a large bowl suitable for microwave cooking, at least 2.2 litres (4 pints) in capacity. Alternatively, use a microwave rice cooker if you have one. Add the coconut liquid, chilli, ginger, curry leaves, turmeric and salt.

- Cover, turning back or puncturing cling film. Cook on high for 6 minutes, then on low for a further 6 minutes.

- Spread the prawns and tomato over the rice. Re-cover the bowl and cook on low for 2½ minutes. Leave to stand for 5 minutes.

- Add the coriander leaves, fork them through the rice, and serve.

CAULIFLOWER AND BROCCOLI IN SPICED ALMOND SAUCE

Although I use a combination of cauliflower and broccoli, you could use double the quantity of one of these vegetables.

SERVES 4

2 tablespoons ghee or unsalted butter
1 onion, finely chopped
175ml (6fl oz) semi-skimmed milk
1 teaspoon Ground Roasted Coriander (see page 13)
½ teaspoon Ground Roasted Cumin (see page 13)
¼ teaspoon ground turmeric
¼ teaspoon freshly ground black pepper

½ teaspoon chilli powder or to taste
¾ teaspoon salt or to taste
225g (8oz) cauliflower, cut into 1cm (½in) florets
225g (8oz) broccoli, cut into 1cm (½in) florets
3 tablespoons ground almonds
2 tablespoons chopped fresh coriander leaves

- Melt the ghee or butter gently in a frying pan on the hob and fry the onion, stirring regularly, for 7–8 minutes until it is tinged with colour.

- Meanwhile, pour the milk into a 1.75 litre (3 pint) casserole or dish suitable for microwave cooking. Add the coriander, cumin, turmeric, pepper and chilli powder. Stir thoroughly, cover and cook on high for 2 minutes.

- Stir in the salt and add the cauliflower and broccoli. Mix well, then cover and cook on high for 5 minutes, stirring halfway through the time.

- Add the ground almonds, mix thoroughly and cook, uncovered, on high for 2½ minutes, stirring and rearranging the vegetables halfway through cooking.

- Stir in the fried onions and coriander leaves, cover and leave to stand for 5–6 minutes before serving.

GINGER, TURMERIC AND CORIANDER RICE

This wonderfully fragrant rice dish will complement almost any curry. It is particularly good with Masala Chicken Livers (see page 89) and looks tempting when the spiced liver is served on a bed of the cooked rice as a complete meal.

SERVES 4

280g (10oz) basmati rice, washed and then soaked in cold water for 15 minutes
600ml (1 pint) boiling water
½ teaspoon ground turmeric
1 bay leaf, crumpled
1cm (½in) cube fresh root ginger, peeled and grated, or 1 teaspoon Ginger Purée (see page 16)

1–2 small green chillies, seeded and finely chopped
1 teaspoon salt or to taste
2 tablespoons roughly chopped fresh coriander leaves

- Drain the rice and put it into a large bowl suitable for microwave cooking, at least 2.2 litres (4 pints) in capacity. Add the remaining ingredients and stir well.

- Cover, turning back or puncturing cling film. Cook on high for 6 minutes, then on low for a further 6 minutes. Leave to stand for 5 minutes, then fork up the rice and serve.

DILL RICE

The distinctive fresh flavour of dill combines with the unique flavour and aroma of basmati rice in a dish that is a treat with all fish, seafood and pulse-based dishes.

SERVES 4

280g (10oz) basmati rice, washed and then soaked for 15 minutes
2.5cm (1in) piece cinnamon stick
1cm (½in) cube fresh root ginger, peeled and grated, or 1 teaspoon Ginger Purée (see page 16)

½ teaspoon ground turmeric
½ teaspoon salt or to taste
2 teaspoons butter
3 tablespoons chopped fresh dill
525ml (18fl oz) hot water

- Drain the rice and put it into a large bowl suitable for microwave cooking, at least 2.2 litres (4 pints) in capacity. Add the remaining ingredients and stir well.

- Cover, turning back or puncturing cling film. Cook on high for 7 minutes, then on low for a further 5 minutes. Leave to stand for 5–6 minutes, then fork up the rice and serve.

PLAIN COOKED BASMATI RICE
To cook plain, unflavoured rice, wash and soak 280g (10oz) rice as above. Drain and place in the bowl, add 525ml (18fl oz) water and stir well. Cover and cook as above. If you want to enliven plain rice slightly, add ½ teaspoon salt and 30g (1oz) butter to the dish with the water. The cooked rice can also be topped with fried onions.

SAFFRON RICE

This classic dish can be cooked with ease in the microwave.

SERVES 4

pinch of saffron strands, pounded
2 tablespoons hot milk
225g (8oz) basmati rice
450ml (15fl oz) boiling water
2.5cm (1in) piece cinnamon stick
4 green cardamom pods, bruised

2 cloves
$\frac{1}{2}$ teaspoon salt or to taste
1 tablespoon butter
To garnish
seeds from $\frac{1}{2}$ pomegranate
snipped fresh chives

- Add the pounded saffron to the hot milk and set aside. Wash the rice, drain and soak in cold water for 15 minutes, then drain thoroughly.

- Put the water, cinnamon, cardamoms and cloves into a microwave rice cooker or large bowl suitable for microwave cooking, at least 2.28 litres (4 pints) in capacity. Cover and cook on high for 4 minutes.

- Add the rice, salt and butter. Stir, cover and cook on high for 4 minutes, then on low for 5 minutes. Sprinkle the saffron-infused milk at random on the surface of the rice, cover and cook on low for 1 minute. Leave to stand for 5 minutes.

- Fluff up the rice with a fork to distribute the saffron-coloured grains among the white grains and create a striking appearance. Transfer the rice to a serving dish. Arrange a neat border of pomegranate seeds around the rice and scatter a few seeds on top, then sprinkle with the chives.

Sweet Treats

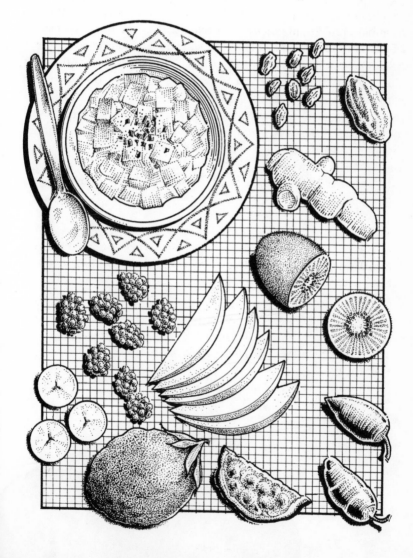

In India, desserts are not usually served, but fresh fruits, fruit salads and chilled, sweetened yogurt normally round off a meal. Sweet dishes are served on special occasions.

If you decide to offer a sweet course other than fruit, then selecting the right kind of dish is just as important as choosing the main course. I find the traditional Indian sweets quite heavy and far too sweet after a large meal. Although these sweets play a major role in Indian cooking, they are associated with festive occasions, celebrations and high teas. India celebrates 13 festivals every 12 months. Sweets are said to be the food of the gods and exchanging sweets during festivals is an old Hindu tradition, so it is easy to understand the importance of these recipes as part of the Indian culinary culture.

Despite tradition, many people (my own family included) find that a meal is not complete without something sweet. I usually experiment with different ideas and in this chapter I have collated a selection of recipes for desserts and sweetmeats that are ideal to round off spicy meals. Most of them are fruit-based and are better, I find, than the slightly heavier dishes, such as the Goan Sweet Potato Cake (see page 204), Banana Halwa (see page 203) and the rice desserts, which I would serve only after a light main course (perhaps to follow a main-course salad).

EXOTIC FRUITS IN CHILLI-FLAVOURED SYRUP

I can imagine the raised eyebrows at the mention of chillies and syrup – but this is not particularly hot. Choose those large, plump and succulent-looking fresh red chillies rather than the thin, long varieties such as Thai or bird's eye chillies. The large chillies are mild and sweet with a distinctive flavour which tastes perfect with the acidity of the fruits in this recipe. Leave the stalks intact on the chillies so that they look quite pretty when served.

SERVES 4

115g (4oz) sugar
6 cloves
5cm (2in) piece cinnamon stick
5mm (¼in) thick slice fresh root ginger
300ml (½ pint) water
400g (14oz) can lychees

1 ripe pineapple, peeled, cored and cut into bite-sized pieces
2–3 large plump fresh red chillies
1 ripe mango, peeled, stoned and cut into bite-sized pieces
2–3 kiwi fruits, peeled and cut into bite-sized pieces

- Put the sugar, cloves, cinnamon and ginger into a saucepan and add the water. Drain the lychees and add the syrup from the can to the syrup; set the fruit aside. Place over medium heat and stir until the sugar has dissolved, then simmer for 10 minutes.

- Add the pineapple to the syrup and cook for 10 minutes, until softened. Add the chillies and simmer for 5–7 minutes.

- Meanwhile, place the mango and kiwi fruit in a large heatproof serving bowl. Add the reserved lychees. Pour the cooked pineapple and its syrup over the fruits and leave to cool completely. Remove the spices and ginger, if you wish, before serving, but pick out the chillies and arrange them on top as a decoration.

SPICED PEACH COMPOTE

Growing up in the foothills of the Himalayas, I enjoyed fruits such as peaches, plums and cherries that are not so readily available in other parts of India. We made use of these fruits in many different sweet and savoury recipes. This simple dessert can also be made with nectarines, or, when you are really short of time, use canned peaches in natural juice.

SERVES 4

6–8 large ripe, firm peaches
300ml (½ pint) water
115g (4oz) soft brown sugar
3 star anise or 4–5 cloves
55g (2oz) seedless raisins

2 tablespoons rose water or brandy
fromage frais or Greek-style yogurt
   to serve
sprigs of fresh mint to decorate

- Put the peaches in a large bowl and cover with boiling water. Leave to soak for 2–3 minutes, then drain, peel and halve the fruit. Discard the stones and cut each peach half into 2–3 slices.

- Put the water, sugar, star anise or cloves and raisins into a saucepan and bring to the boil. Add the peach slices and cook for 5–6 minutes, until softened. Remove from the heat and leave to cool.

- Stir in the rose water or brandy and serve topped with fromage frais or Greek yogurt. Decorate with sprigs of mint.

SPICED MANGO WITH COINTREAU CREAM

Mangoes are meant to evoke romance, and legend has it that lovers often met under mango trees on moonlit nights! Perhaps this is the dessert to complete a romantic Valentine's Day dinner.

SERVES 4

4 firm ripe mangoes
½ teaspoon ground ginger
½ teaspoon ground cinnamon
250g (9oz) crème fraîche

30g (1oz) icing sugar
1 tablespoon orange juice
1 tablespoon Cointreau
finely grated rind of 1 orange

- Peel the mangoes and slice the flesh off the stone as close as possible, then cut into bite-sized pieces. Divide the mango among individual serving dishes and sprinkle with the ginger and cinnamon.

- Beat the creme fraîche with a fork, gradually adding the icing sugar, orange juice, Cointreau and grated orange rind. Pile the crème fraîche mixture on the mango. Chill before serving.

CARROT AND CARDAMOM DESSERT

This dessert is simple, speedy and superb.

SERVES 4

55g (2oz) ghee or unsalted butter
5cm (2in) piece cinnamon stick,
  halved
450g (1lb) carrots, grated
30g (1oz) seedless raisins
85g (3oz) caster sugar

finely grated rind of 1 large orange
juice of ½ large orange
1 teaspoon ground cardamom seeds
To serve
crème fraîche
grated nutmeg

- Melt the ghee or butter gently in a heavy-based saucepan. Add the cinnamon and cook gently for 20–25 seconds, then add the carrots. Increase the heat to medium and fry, stirring regularly, for 5 minutes.

- Stir in the raisins and sugar. Continue to cook for 6–8 minutes. Stir in the orange rind and juice, and the ground cardamom, then remove from the heat. Leave to cool.

- Serve topped with crème fraîche, sprinkled with a little nutmeg.

CARAMELIZED CREAMED RICE WITH DRIED FRUITS AND NUTS

This very quick recipe is based on a childhood favourite of mine, prepared by my mother on special occasions and served in a decorative silver bowl. The slow-cooked white rice pudding was dotted with plump, juicy sultanas and crushed pistachio nuts. I have adapted the recipe by using canned rice pudding and topping the dessert with caramelized sugar.

SERVES 4

1 tablespoon ghee or unsalted butter
4 green cardamom pods, bruised
5cm (2in) piece cinnamon stick
1 bay leaf, crumbled
1 tablespoon chopped blanched almonds

2 tablespoons sultanas
625g (1lb 6oz) can creamed rice
150ml (5fl oz) milk
150ml (5fl oz) double cream
4 tablespoons demerara sugar
1 tablespoon shelled unsalted pistachio nuts

- Preheat the grill to high. Melt the ghee or butter in a heavy-based saucepan over gentle heat. Add the cardamoms, cinnamon and bay leaf. Fry the flavouring ingredients gently for 30–35 seconds, then add the almonds and sultanas. Stir until the sultanas are puffed.

- Add the creamed rice, milk and cream. Stir over medium heat for 5–6 minutes, until the rice is piping hot.

- Transfer the pudding to a flameproof serving dish and sprinkle the sugar thickly over the top. Place under the grill until the sugar is caramelized, then set aside to cool. Chill the caramelized rice for several hours.

- Toast the pistachio nuts under the grill on a low setting. Cool and lightly crush the nuts, then sprinkle them over the dessert just before serving.

SWEET POTATO PUDDING WITH SEASONAL FRUITS

Sweet potatoes are versatile ingredients and here they make a change from dairy products, the popular base for so many Indian sweet dishes. Serve any seasonal fruit to bring contrast of flavour and colour to the dessert. Mango, kiwi fruit and pomegranate seeds make a delightful combination, or try mixed berries, such as strawberries, blackberries and blueberries.

SERVES 4

30g (1oz) ghee or unsalted butter
6 green cardamom pods, bruised
400g (14oz) sweet potatoes, peeled and grated
150ml (5fl oz) milk

75–85g (2½–3oz) caster sugar
400g (14fl oz) evaporated milk
2 tablespoons rose water
fresh fruit to serve

- Melt the ghee or unsalted butter in a heavy-based saucepan over gentle heat. Add and fry the cardamoms until they are puffed, then stir in the sweet potatoes. Add the fresh milk and sugar, and cook over medium heat until the sugar has dissolved.

- Pour in the evaporated milk and bring to a gentle simmer over medium heat. Cook, uncovered, for 20–25 minutes. Stir occasionally during the first half of the cooking time, then more frequently during the last 8–10 minutes to ensure that the thickened milk does not stick to the pan. Turn the heat down to low at this stage.

- Stir in the rose water and transfer the mixture to a serving dish or individual glass bowls, then cool and chill for at least 1 hour. Top with mixed fresh fruit and serve.

BANANA HALWA

Offer this simple sweetmeat with coffee at the end of a meal.

SERVES 4–5

2–3 tablespoons pine nuts	55–75g (2–2½oz) sugar
85g (3oz) ghee or unsalted butter	½ teaspoon grated nutmeg
85g (3oz) semolina	½ teaspoon ground cinnamon
30g (1oz) seedless raisins	400g (14oz) can evaporated milk
3 large bananas	finely grated rind of 1 large orange

- Dry roast the pine nuts until they are lightly browned, then set aside to cool. Lightly crush the pine nuts by placing them in a plastic bag and using a rolling pin, or do this in a coffee grinder.

- Melt the ghee or butter gently in a heavy-based frying pan. Add the semolina and stir-fry over medium heat for 4–5 minutes. Add the raisins and continue to stir-fry for a further 2–3 minutes, until the semolina is golden brown. Remove from the heat.

- Peel and finely chop the bananas. Add to the semolina and return the pan to the heat. Stir in the sugar, nutmeg, cinnamon, evaporated milk and orange rind. Cook over medium heat, stirring, for 3–4 minutes or until the mixture is the consistency of a soft dough and it comes away from the sides and bottom of the pan.

- Lightly grease a large plate and spread the mixture on it, then use a metal spoon or plastic spatula to shape it into a large square. Push the sides inwards and level the top neatly.

- Sprinkle the crushed pine nuts on top and press them gently into the halwa. Leave to cool completely, then cut into squares or diamonds to serve.

GOAN SWEET POTATO CAKE

Use orange-fleshed sweet potatoes for this moist-textured cake. The potatoes should be fairly dry when mashed, so steam them or cook them in the microwave. You can boil them in their skins, but I prefer to chop them and cook them in the microwave.

SERVES 6

375g (13oz) sweet potatoes, peeled and cut into 2.5cm (1in) cubes
115g (4oz) softened butter or margarine
140g (5oz) caster sugar
2 large eggs, beaten
115g (4oz) self-raising flour

$\frac{1}{2}$ teaspoon baking powder
1 teaspoon ground cinnamon
3 tablespoons orange juice
icing sugar to dust
crème fraîche or fromage frais to serve

- Place the sweet potatoes in a bowl or casserole suitable for use in the microwave and add 2–3 tablespoons water. Cover and microwave on high for 5 minutes. Mash the potatoes and set aside to cool.

- Preheat the oven to 190°C/375°F/Gas 5. Line a 20cm (8in) cake tin with baking parchment. Grease the parchment and dust it lightly with flour.

- Beat the butter or margarine with the sugar until soft and fluffy. Mix in the beaten egg a little at a time.

- Sift the flour, baking powder and cinnamon together. Stir into the mixture and add the orange juice. Mix until all the ingredients are thoroughly combined, then pour into the prepared tin.

- Bake in the centre of the oven for 40–45 minutes until the cake is risen, golden brown and firm to the touch.

- Allow the cake to cool in the tin for 10 minutes, then turn it out on to a wire rack. Dust the hot cake generously with icing sugar and leave to cool. Cut into slices and serve with crème fraîche or fromage frais.

SPICED YOGURT IN BRANDY-SNAP BASKETS

This recipe is based on the traditional west Indian dish known as shrikand. For the traditional version, the yogurt is tied up in muslin and strained for 4–5 hours. A combination of Greek-style yogurt and curd cheese gives a similar result. In India, shrikand is served with puris (deep-fried puffed bread) and eaten during the meal. However, because of its refreshing taste and the fact that it is easily digested, I prefer to serve it as a dessert. The spiced yogurt can also be served on its own, scattered with nuts, or used to fill a sweet pastry case.

SERVES 6

pinch of saffron strands, pounded
2 tablespoons hot milk
200g (7oz) Greek-style yogurt
200g (7oz) curd cheese
55g (2oz) caster sugar

$1/2$ teaspoon ground cardamom seeds
$1/2$ teaspoon freshly grated nutmeg
To serve
6 brandy-snap baskets
fresh fruits of your choice

- Soak the saffron in the hot milk for 10–15 minutes. Stir the saffron liquid with the remaining ingredients until thoroughly combined and chill for about 1 hour.

- Pile the spiced yogurt mixture into the brandy-snap baskets and top with fresh fruit, then serve at once. If the baskets are allowed to stand for any length of time they will soften.

COOK'S TIP
You can use a few drops of vanilla essence instead of saffron. Grinding a small quantity of cardamom seeds in a coffee mill is easier if you add the required quantity of sugar (or part of the weighed amount) needed for the recipe.

GINGER ICE CREAM WITH TAMARIND SAUCE

Tangy tamarind sauce complements the zingy ginger ice cream, which could not be easier to make. The combination of ginger and tamarind is also a perfect aid to digestion.

MAKES 1.2 LITRES (2 PINTS)

300ml (½ pint) double cream
400g (14oz) can sweetened
   condensed milk
1½ teaspoons ground ginger
4 large egg whites

For the tamarind sauce
55g (2oz) stoned dried dates
1 rounded teaspoon tamarind
   concentrate
175ml (6fl oz) boiling water
1 tablespoon crystallized ginger to
   serve

- To make the ice cream, whip the cream until thick, but not stiff. Gradually beat in the condensed milk. Blend the ground ginger with a little water and beat it gently into the cream mixture.

- Whisk the egg whites until they stand in soft peaks, then fold them into the mixture using a metal spoon. Pour the mixture into an ice-cream churn and freeze following the manufacturer's instructions. Alternatively, place in a suitable freezer container and freeze for at least 5 hours, or until firm.

- To make the tamarind sauce, soak the dates and tamarind in the water for 15–20 minutes, then purée in a food processor or blender. Transfer to a bowl and chill. This sauce keeps well in a covered container in the refrigerator for up to a week.

- Soften the ice cream for 30–35 minutes in the refrigerator before serving, if necessary. Arrange scoops in glass dishes and top with crystallized ginger. Pour a little tamarind sauce around the ice cream and serve.

Menu Planner

The following menus, each with a preparation plan, are intended as a guide to saving time when preparing and cooking complete meals. Selecting a practical combination of dishes and cooking them in the right order makes the best use of every minute in the kitchen. Besides showing how to save time, the menus illustrate the idea of choosing complementary dishes, rather than clashing flavours. Making sure that everyday meals are nutritionally balanced is important, but relax when entertaining or planning a menu for a special occasion – we should all let ourselves go once in a while!

In India, most of the alcohol is consumed before dinner and the food is generally accompanied by water. Europeans seem to prefer light beer with Indian food, but wine does complement spicy food if you choose the right type. I am not a connoisseur of wine, but over the years, by trial and error, I have come to rely on the following principle.

Choose the wine according to the strength of the sauce, not the colour of the meat. I find that many white wines complement spiced dishes. Australian or New Zealand Chardonnay with prominent oak flavours; dry sparkling wines or champagne; Alsace wines; Californian Chenin Blanc; Italian Frascati; or Soave all work extremely well. Highly spiced, full-flavoured dishes take red wines, such as Australian Shiraz; a good Cabernet Sauvignon; Rioja Reserva; Beaujolais Villages; or a red Bordeaux.

MENU 1

This substantial and nourishing family meal is full of complementary ingredients. The aroma and flavour of basmati rice are perfect with both the main dish and the spiced aubergines. The dessert is light and luscious, with palate-refreshing flavours from the orange rind and juice.

KOFTAS IN HOT LENTIL SAUCE
ROASTED SPICED AUBERGINE
BOILED BASMATI RICE

CARROT AND CARDAMOM DESSERT

PREPARATION PLAN

- Wash the lentils and leave to drain. Wash and soak the rice.

- Prepare and start cooking the koftas. While they are cooking, preheat the oven for the aubergines.

- Make the dessert while the koftas are cooking, then leave to cool.

- Slice and fry the onions for the koftas.

- While the onions are frying, drain and cook the rice either on the hob or in the microwave.

- While the rice is cooking, prepare the aubergines and place in the oven. Finish cooking the koftas.

MENU 2

This two-course menu is ideal when you want to round off a busy working day with a delicious meal that is simple to cook. The light tomato, black pepper and coriander sauce served with the chicken is complemented by the rich sunflower-seed and coconut sauce with the sweetcorn.

CHICKEN IN TOMATO, BLACK PEPPER AND CORIANDER SAUCE
SWEETCORN IN SUNFLOWER AND COCONUT SAUCE
BASIC CHAPATIS OR EASY NAAN

SPICED YOGURT IN BRANDY-SNAP BASKETS

PREPARATION PLAN

- If you already have chapatis or naan in the freezer, you can put this meal together in just 45 minutes.

- Start by making the dough for the chapatis or naan.

- While the dough is resting, prepare the ingredients for the chicken dish and put it on to cook.

- Make the sweetcorn dish while the chicken is cooking for 25 minutes.

- Mix the yogurt for the dessert, cover and chill until ready to serve. Spoon the yogurt into the brandy-snap baskets when you are about to serve them.

- Cook the chapatis or naan and serve the meal.

MENU 3

This vegetarian meal looks good and tastes great, as well as providing all the essential nutrients for a well-balanced diet. The pilau is particularly delicious with the raita and because the main course is not too filling, everyone will have room to enjoy the substantial and scrumptious sweet potato cake.

CARROT, SPINACH AND CHICK-PEA PILAU
ONION RAITA WITH ROASTED PEANUTS
OR
COCONUT-COATED CUCUMBER WITH MUSTARD AND LIME
PAPPADUMS (OPTIONAL)

GOAN SWEET POTATO CAKE

PREPARATION PLAN

- Preheat the oven for the cake. Mix the cake while the oven is heating, then bake it. Continue preparing the meal while the cake is baking.

- Wash and soak the rice for the pilau.

- Mix the yogurt and the other ingredients for the raita, but do not sprinkle with the peanuts and spices. Chill the raita. Crush the peanuts and set aside.

- If you are making the cucumber dish, chop the cucumber, then grind and mix the coconut and chillies. Set aside.

- Prepare the vegetables for the pilau. Drain and cook the rice. While the onions are frying for the pilau, grill, fry or microwave the pappadums (if serving).

- Finish cooking the pilau. Add the finishing touches to the raita or to the cucumber.

MENU 4

This is a fun meal to impress friends, with a popular combination for the starter and slightly unusual dishes to follow. Both kheema naan and the vegetable cakes are filling, so the light fruit dessert is ideal as it has a pleasing acidity that cuts the spiciness of the first courses.

KHEEMA NAAN
PAPPADUMS
MINT AND YOGURT CHUTNEY

SMOKED MACKEREL ON SPICY VEGETABLE CAKES

EXOTIC FRUITS IN CHILLI-FLAVOURED SYRUP

PREPARATION PLAN

- Make the dessert and leave to cool. Blend the chutney ingredients, cover and chill, if liked, or set aside.

- Prepare the vegetable cakes.

- Prepare the smoked mackerel mixture and set aside in the refrigerator. Prepare and chill the salad ingredients.

- Prepare the kheema naan ready to grill. Preheat the grill.

- Fry the vegetable cakes, then keep them hot in a cool oven.

- Grill the pappadums first, then the kheema naan.

MENU 5

This is an excellent menu for entertaining because both the dessert and the raita are prepared in advance, leaving you free to chat to friends before the meal. The creamy turkey main dish is fabulous with richly fragrant saffron rice, and the exciting, sophisticated dessert brings the menu to a fitting close.

PRAWN PURI

BREAST OF TURKEY IN SOURED CREAM AND CORIANDER SAUCE
SAFFRON RICE
BROCCOLI AND RED PEPPER RAITA

GINGER ICE CREAM WITH TAMARIND SAUCE

PREPARATION PLAN

- Make the ice cream a day or two in advance. Make the tamarind sauce in advance and store it in the refrigerator.
- Prepare and cook the turkey.
- While the turkey is cooking, soak the rice. Soak the saffron.
- Cook the vegetables and spices for the raita.
- Cook the prawns and keep hot. Arrange the naan or pitta bread on a grill pan, ready to grill.
- Drain and cook the rice. This does not need any attention and will keep hot for at least 30 minutes when cooked.
- Preheat the grill for the naan or pitta bread. Add the finishing touches to the turkey and keep hot.
- Grill the naan or pitta bread and serve the first course.
- Before you serve the main course, place the ice cream in the refrigerator.
- Finish mixing the raita and serve the main course.

MENU 6

This menu takes slightly longer, but it's worth it: the contrasting flavours complement one another beautifully.

GOLDEN SWEET POTATO SOUP

PAN-FRIED LAMB CUTLETS WITH SPICY GREEN PEA SAUCE
SAFFRON RICE
OR
EASY NAAN
CAULIFLOWER AND POTATOES WITH AROMATIC SPICES
FRESH PLUM CHUTNEY

SPICED PEACH COMPOTE

PREPARATION PLAN

- Make the plum chutney well in advance.
- Marinate the lamb cutlets. Make the dessert and leave to cool.
- Wash and soak the rice/make the bread dough and leave to rest.
- Make the soup. While it is simmering, boil the potatoes for the cauliflower and potato dish and leave to cool.
- Cook and cool the cauliflower. While the cauliflower is cooking, make the green pea sauce for the lamb.
- Finish the soup and keep hot or reheat it just before serving. If you are making naan, preheat the grill and prepare the grill pan.
- If you are cooking rice, place it in the microwave.
- Cook the lamb cutlets and finish cooking the cauliflower and potato dish.
- If making the naan, cook them while the lamb is cooking.

MENU 7

Holidays are meant for fun and good food. This is the ideal menu for relaxed days with family or friends. Tangy rhubarb chutney is scrumptious with turkey pakoras, and the tomato raita laced with spice is the perfect foil for sausage pilau. Serving a cold dessert allows you to enjoy a leisurely pause between courses before appreciating the heady bouquet of ripe mango and zesty Cointreau.

TURKEY PAKORAS
RHUBARB CHUTNEY WITH ROASTED CUMIN

HOT SAUSAGE PILAU
TOMATO RAITA
GRILLED OR FRIED PAPPADUMS (OPTIONAL)

SPICED MANGO WITH COINTREAU CREAM

PREPARATION PLAN

- Make the chutney well in advance as it will keep for up to 2 weeks.
- Prepare the turkey for the pakoras, cover and chill. Wash and soak the rice.
- Prepare the mangoes and chill. Prepare the Cointreau cream and chill.
- Make the raita, cover and chill. Grill, fry or microwave the pappadums (if serving).
- Grill the sausages for the pilau. Drain the rice and make the pilau.
- When the pilau has been cooking for 6–7 minutes, finish making the pakoras. Heat the oil for deep-frying and make the batter. Fry the pakoras. Leave the pilau to rest while the first course is served.

MENU 8

This is a protein-packed family meal with a light main course and a carbohydrate-based rice dessert. The dessert is ready in just 10 minutes, then it should be cooled and chilled, so it is an ideal recipe for making early in the day or a day ahead when you have a few minutes to spare.

SPICED SCRAMBLED EGGS WITH KING PRAWNS
EASY NAAN
POTATO AND POMEGRANATE RAITA

CARAMELIZED CREAMED RICE WITH DRIED FRUITS AND NUTS

PREPARATION PLAN

- Make the dessert well in advance. Toast and crush the nuts in advance.

- Make the naan dough.

- While the dough is resting, cook the potatoes and leave to cool. Peel the pomegranate and remove the seeds.

- Preheat the grill for the naan. Roll out and cook the naan, then keep them hot.

- Assemble the raita and sprinkle the nuts on the dessert.

- Cook the scrambled eggs and prawns. Serve the meal.

Suppliers of Indian Ingredients

AVON
Bart Spices Ltd
York Road
Bedminster
Bristol BS3 4AD
Tel: 0117 977 3474
Fax: 0117 972 0216
(Also provide mail order service)

EDINBURGH
Nastiuks (wholesaler)
1 Garden Field
Nine Mile Burn
A702
South of Edinburgh
Midlothian EH26 9LT
Tel: 01968 679 333

GLASGOW
Oriental Food Stores
303–5 Great Western Road
Glasgow G4 9HS
Tel: 0141 334 8133

HUMBERSIDE
Indian and Continental Food
   Stores
69 Princes Avenue
Hull HU5 3QN
Tel: 01482 346 915

LONDON
Patel Brothers
187–9 Upper Tooting Road
London SW17 7TG
Tel: 020 8767 6338

Dadu's Ltd
190–198 Upper Tooting Road
London SW17 7EW
Tel: 020 8672 4984

Asian Food Centre
540-544 Harrow Road
Maida Vale
London W9 3GG
Tel: 020 8960 3731

MIDDLESEX
Asian Food Centre
175–77 Staines Road
Hounslow
Middlesex TW3 3JB
Tel: 020 8570 7346

Ealing Road shops
100–200 Ealing Road
Wembley
Middlesex

Dadoos
off Ealing Road, Wembley
(near Alperton Bus Station)

Gifto Cash and Carry
115–119 The Broadway
Southall
Middlesex UB1 1LW
Tel: 020 8574 8602

SURREY
Spicyfoods Cash and Carry
460 London Road
Croydon
Surrey CR0 2SS
Tel: 020 8684 9844

Atif's Superstore
103 Walton Road
Woking
Surrey GU21 5DW
Tel: 01483 762 774

YORKSHIRE
Bhullar Brothers Ltd
44 Springwood Street
Huddersfield
W. Yorkshire HD1 4BE
Tel: 01484 531 607

MAIL ORDER

Fox's Spices
Unit J and K
Mason's Road Industrial Estate
Stratford-upon-Avon
Warwickshire CV37 9NF
Tel: 01789 266 420
Fax: 01789 267 737

Natco Spices
T. Choithram and Sons (Stores)
   Ltd
Choithram House
Lancelot Road
Wembley
Middlesex HA0 2BG
Tel: 020 8903 8311
Fax: 020 8900 1426

ON LINE
www.exotic spice.co.uk

Index

almonds: caramelized creamed rice with dried fruits and nuts, 201
  cauliflower and broccoli in spiced almond sauce, 191
  chicken korma with whole spices, 78-9
aniseed, 20
apple and coconut chutney, 173
asafoetida, 20, 168
aubergines: roasted spiced aubergines, 156
  spiced aubergine purée with eggs, 132
avocado, paneer and mango salad, 144

baby corn and chick-pea korma, 122
bacon omelette, 111
banana halwa, 203
bay leaves, 20
beans and mushrooms in chilli tomato sauce, 126
Bengal tarka dhal, 124
besan, 20
bhajiyas, courgette, 45
bird's eye chillies, 22
brandy-snap baskets, spiced yogurt in, 205
breads, 11-12, 160
  chapatis, 162-3
  easy naan, 166
  fenugreek and chilli chapatis, 164
  kheema naan, 39
  khurmi naan, 167
  mint and coriander chapatis, 165
  prawn puri, 35
broccoli: broccoli and red pepper raita, 174
  cauliflower and broccoli in spiced almond sauce, 191
burgers, tuna, 60
butter: butter sauce, 18
  ghee, 23-4
butternut squash: spicy squash slices, 46

cabbage, braised with mustard and fenugreek, 153
cake, Goan sweet potato, 204

canned foods, 12
caramelized creamed rice with dried fruits and nuts, 201
cardamom, 20-1
  carrot and cardamom dessert, 200
carrots: carrot and cardamom dessert, 200
  carrot, spinach and chick-pea pilau, 120
  carrots in spicy split-pea sauce, 155
  chicken in golden carrot sauce, 66
  white radish and carrot raita, 178
cashew nuts: chicken with vegetable medley, 76-7
  fish korma, 52
  pineapple chutney, 171
  Quorn kababs, 42
  roasting, 77
cauliflower: cauliflower and broccoli in spiced almond sauce, 191
  cauliflower and potatoes with aromatic spices, 150
channa dhal, 26
  carrots in spicy split-pea sauce, 155
  masala channa dhal with courgettes, 123
  tarka channa dhal, 125
chapati flour, 21
chapatis, 11
  basic, 162-3
  fenugreek and chilli, 164
  mint and coriander, 165
cheese: egg koftas, 43
  khurmi naan, 167
  see also paneer
chick peas: baby corn and chick-pea korma, 122
  carrot, spinach and chick-pea pilau, 120
  chilli, lime and coriander chick peas, 158
  tangy potato and chick-pea salad, 137
chicken: chicken and mushrooms in a hot tomato sauce, 184-5
  chicken cutlets, 81
  chicken in coconut and fresh coriander chutney, 70-1
  chicken in golden carrot sauce, 66
  chicken in tomato, black pepper and coriander sauce, 68-9

chicken *continued*
chicken jhal frazie, 82-3
chicken korma with whole spices, 78-9
chicken madras, 65
chicken masala, 75
chicken mulligatawny, 32
chicken pasanda, 88
chicken pilau, 86-7
chicken shahi korma, 186-7
chicken with vegetable medley, 76-7
dry-spiced chicken, 72
fried chilli chicken with coconut and
curry leaves, 67
meatballs and new potatoes in spiced
yogurt, 138-9
minced chicken and vegetable bhuna, 80
pineapple salad with chicken bhuna,
140-1
quick chicken tikka masala, 72-3
tamarind chicken, 74
see also poussins
chillies, 21-2
beans and mushrooms in chilli tomato
sauce, 126
chilli, lime and coriander chick peas, 158
exotic fruits in chilli-flavoured syrup,
197
fenugreek and chilli chapatis, 164
fried chilli chicken with coconut and
curry leaves, 67
fried pork with dill and chillies, 97
garlic potatoes with chilli and mustard,
147
khurmi naan, 167
minced lamb with garlic, chilli and eggs,
104-5
northern curry sauce, 19
spicy meatloaf with chilli tomato sauce,
100-1
tamarind-coated trout with chilli tomato
sauce, 54
chutneys: apple and coconut, 173
coconut and fresh coriander, 70-1
mint and yogurt, 169
pineapple, 171
plum, 172
rhubarb with roasted cumin, 170
cinnamon, 22
cloves, 22
coconut, 22
apple and coconut chutney, 173
chicken in coconut and fresh coriander
chutney, 70-1

chutney *continued*
chunky tomatoes in mellow coconut
sauce, 154
coconut-coated cucumber with mustard
and lime, 145
fried chilli chicken with coconut and
curry leaves, 67
peas in coconut and roasted cumin
sauce, 152
sweetcorn in sunflower and coconut
sauce, 151
tomato and coconut rice with prawns,
190
coconut milk: eggs in curry-leaf coconut
milk, 129
mashed potato with mustard-speckled
coconut milk, 148
prawns in coconut milk, 183
prawns, lentils and green beans in
coconut milk, 59
cod masala, 49
cod's roe, spiced, 61
cook-ahead sauces, 16-17
coriander leaves: breast of turkey in
soured cream and coriander sauce, 92-3
chicken in coconut and fresh coriander
chutney, 70-1
chilli, lime and coriander chick peas,
158
egg koftas, 43
ginger, turmeric and coriander rice, 192
mint and coriander chapatis, 165
sweet potato cakes, 44
tomato and coriander soup, 29
coriander seeds, 22
chicken in tomato, black pepper and
coriander sauce, 68-9
ground roasted coriander, 13
courgettes: courgette bhajiyas, 45
masala channa dhal with, 123
cucumber: coconut-coated cucumber with
mustard and lime, 145
cumin, 22
ground roasted cumin, 13
peas in coconut and roasted cumin
sauce, 152
rhubarb chutney with roasted cumin,
170
curries: chicken madras, 65
chicken masala, 75
cod masala, 49
madras fish curry, 50
northern curry sauce, 19

curry leaves, 22
eggs in curry-leaf coconut milk, 129
fried chilli chicken with coconut and
curry leaves, 67
madras curry sauce, 17
radish raita, 176

dates: ginger ice cream with tamarind
sauce, 206
dhal, 25, 26
Bengal tarka dhal, 124
Masala channa dhal with courgettes, 123
prawns, lentils and green beans in
coconut milk, 59
tarka channa dhal, 125
dill: dill rice, 193
fried pork with dill and chillies, 97

eggs: bacon omelette, 111
egg koftas, 43
egg pilau, 130-1
eggs in curry-leaf coconut milk, 129
grilled mushroom omelette, 133
minced lamb with garlic, chilli and eggs,
104-5
spiced aubergine purée with eggs, 132
spiced prawns with fried eggs, 58
spiced scrambled eggs with king
prawns, 57
spicy potato fingers with whole eggs, 128
exotic fruits in chilli-flavoured syrup, 197

fennel seeds, 23
fenugreek leaves, 23
fenugreek and chilli chapatis, 164
fenugreek seeds, 23
braised cabbage with mustard and
fenugreek, 153
fish and shellfish, 47-62
fish and seafood spice blend, 15
madras fish curry, 50
see also individual types of fish
five-spice mix, 13
fruit: exotic fruits in chilli-flavoured
syrup, 197
sweet potato pudding with seasonal
fruits, 202

garam masala, 23
garlic, 23
garlic potatoes with chilli and mustard,
147
madras curry sauce, 17

garlic continued
minced lamb with garlic, chilli and eggs,
104-5
northern curry sauce, 19
prawn balchao, 168
purée, 8, 16
ghee, 23-4
ginger, 24
ginger ice cream with tamarind sauce,
206
ginger, turmeric and coriander rice, 192
purée, 8, 16
spinach and potato soup with fresh
ginger, 30-1
Goan sweet potato cake, 204
green beans, prawns and lentils in
coconut milk, 59

haddock: fish pakoras, 51
halwa, banana, 203

ice cream, ginger, 206
ingredients, 11-13, 20-6

kababs: minced lamb, 38
paneer stuffed with dried prunes, 40-1
Quorn, 42
kadhai sauce, 19
kheema naan, 39
khurmi naan, 167
kidney beans: beans and mushrooms in
chilli tomato sauce, 126
koftas: egg, 43
in hot lentil sauce, 102-3
prawn, 36
korma: baby corn and chick-pea, 122
chicken with whole spices, 78-9
chicken shahi, 186-7
fish, 52

lamb: dry-fried minced lamb with spinach
and tomato, 106-7
kheema naan, 39
koftas in hot lentil sauce, 102-3
minced lamb with garlic, chilli and eggs,
104-5
minced lamb kababs, 38
pan-fried lamb cutlets with spicy green
pea sauce, 98-9
spicy meatloaf with chilli tomato sauce,
100-1
lentils, red, 25
Bengal tarka dhal, 124

lentils, red, *continued*
  koftas in hot lentil sauce, 102-3
  prawns, lentils and green beans in
    coconut milk, 59
liver: lamb's liver with spiced butter, 110
  liver do-piaza, 108-9
  masala chicken livers, 89

mackerel: smoked mackerel on spicy
    vegetable cakes, 62
  spiced mackerel fillets, 56
madras curry sauce, 17
madras fish curry, 50
mangoes: paneer, avocado and mango
    salad, 144
  spiced mango with Cointreau cream,
    199
meat and pulses spice blend, 15
meatballs and new potatoes in spiced
    yogurt, 138-9
meatloaf with chilli tomato sauce, 100-1
microwave cooking, 9-10, 181-94
mint, 24
  mint and coriander chapatis, 165
  mint and yogurt chutney, 169
moong dhal: moong dhal pilau, 117
  prawns, lentils and green beans in
    coconut milk, 59
  turkey simmered in masala dhal, 90-1
mushrooms: beans and mushrooms in
    chilli tomato sauce, 126
  chicken and mushrooms in a hot tomato
    sauce, 184-5
  grilled mushroom omelette, 133
mustard seeds, 24
  braised cabbage with mustard and
    fenugreek, 153
  coconut-coated cucumber with mustard
    and lime, 145
  garlic potatoes with chilli and mustard,
    147
  mashed potato with mustard-speckled
    coconut milk, 148

naan breads: easy naan, 166
  kheema naan, 39
  khurmi naan, 167
northern curry sauce, 19
nutmeg, 24

okra, deep-fried spiced, 157
omelettes: bacon, 111
  grilled mushroom, 133

onion seeds, 24
onions, 24
  liver do-piaza, 108-9
  northern curry sauce, 19
  onion raita with roasted peanuts, 177

pakoras: fish, 51
  potato pakora salad, 142-3
  turkey, 37
pancakes, wholewheat, 161
paneer, 25
  grilled paneer masala with garden peas,
    127
  paneer, avocado and mango salad, 144
  paneer kababs stuffed with dried prunes,
    40-1
pappadums, 11
paprika, 25
peach compote, spiced, 198
peanuts: onion raita with roasted peanuts,
    177
peas: golden semolina pilau, 118-19
  grilled paneer masala with garden peas,
    127
  pan-fried lamb cutlets with spicy green
    pea sauce, 98-9
  peas in coconut and roasted cumin
    sauce, 152
peppercorns, 20
peppers: broccoli and red pepper raita, 174
pickles, 11
pilau *see* rice
pine nuts, poussins with poppy seeds and,
    84-5
pineapple: pineapple chutney, 171
  pineapple salad with chicken bhuna,
    140-1
plums: fresh plum chutney, 172
pomegranate and potato raita, 179
poppy seeds, 25
  poussins with pine nuts and, 84-5
  rainbow trout with poppy-seed sauce,
    55
  roasting, 77
pork: fried pork with dill and chillies, 97
pork sausages in hot tomato sauce, 114
potatoes: breast of turkey in soured cream
    and coriander sauce, 92-3
  cauliflower and potatoes with aromatic
    spices, 150
  eggs in curry-leaf coconut milk, 129
  garlic potatoes with chilli and mustard,
    147

Real Fast Indian Food